THE WILD ELEPHANT
&
THE METHOD OF CAPTURING AND TAMING IT IN CEYLON

AN ELEPHANT CORRAL.

THE WILD ELEPHANT & THE METHOD OF CAPTURING AND TAMING IT IN CEYLON

J. EMERSON TENNENT

GYAN

Published by

Gyan Publishing House
5, Ansari Road
Daryaganj, New Delhi-110002
Phone: 011-47034999, 9811692060
E-mail: books@gyanbooks.com

Distribution Network
gyanbooks.com
India, USA, Canada, UK, Australia, France

ISBN : 978-81-212-4221-9 (PB)
First Published, London, 1867

2nd Impression 2020

Printed at: Gyan Press, Delhi.

The Wild Elephant
&
The Method of Capturing and Taming it in Ceylon
Author: J. Emerson Tennent

THE

WILD ELEPHANT

AND

THE METHOD OF CAPTURING

AND TAMING IT IN

CEYLON.

SIR J. EMERSON TENNENT BART.

K.C.S. LL.D. F.R.S. &c.

AUTHOR OF "CEYLON, AN ACCOUNT OF THE ISLAND,
PHYSICAL, HISTORICAL, AND TOPOGRAPHICAL,"
ETC.

LONDON:
LONGMANS, GREEN, AND CO
1867.

TO

MY INTELLIGENT COMPANION

IN MANY OF THE JOURNEYS THROUGHOUT THE MOUNTAINS AND FORESTS OF CEYLON, IN THE COURSE OF WHICH MUCH OF THE INFORMATION CONTAINED IN THIS VOLUME WAS COLLECTED;

TO

MAJOR SKINNER

CHIEF COMMISSIONER OF ROADS AND PUBLIC WORKS, ETC. ETC.

ONE OF THE MOST EXPERIENCED AND VALUABLE SERVANTS OF THE CROWN;

IT IS INSCRIBED,

IN THE HOPE THAT IT MAY RECALL TO HIM THE PLEASANT MEMORIES WHICH IT AWAKES IN ME.

PREFACE.

In this volume, the chapters descriptive of the structure and habits of the wild elephant are reprinted for the sixth time from a larger work,[1] published originally in 1859. Since the appearance of the First Edition, many corrections and much additional matter have been supplied to me, chiefly from India and Ceylon, and will be found embodied in the following pages.

To one of these in particular I feel bound to direct attention. In the course of a more enlarged essay on the zoology of Ceylon,[2] amongst other proofs of a geological origin for that island, distinct from that of the adjacent continent of India, as evidenced by peculiarities in the flora and fauna of each respectively, I had occasion to advert to a discovery which had been recently an-

[1] *Ceylon:* An Account of the Island, Physical, Historical, and Topographical. 2 vols. 8vo. London, Longmans & Co. 1859.

[2] *Sketches of the Natural History of Ceylon.* London, 1861. See also *Ceylon, etc.* by Sir J. Emerson Tennent. London, 1860, vol. I. pp. 7, 13, 85, 160, 183, &c.

nounced by Temminck in his *Survey of the Dutch possessions in the Indian Archipelago*,[1] that the elephant which abounds in Sumatra (although unknown in the adjacent island of Java), and which had theretofore been regarded as identical in species with the Indian one, has been found to possess peculiarities, in which it differs as much from the elephant of India as the latter does from its African congener. On this new species, to which the natives give the name of "*gadjah*," TEMMINCK has conferred the scientific designation of the *Elephas Sumatranus.* The points which entitle it to this distinction he enumerates minutely in the work[2] before alluded to, and they have been summarized as follows by Prince Lucien Bonaparte.

"This species is perfectly intermediate between the Indian and African, especially in the shape of the skull, and will certainly put an end to the distinction between *Elephas* and *Loxodon*, with those who admit that anatomical genus; since although the crowns of the teeth of *E. Sumatranus* are more like the Asiatic animal, still the less numerous undulated ribbons of enamel are nearly quite as wide as those forming the lozenges of the African. The number of pairs of false ribs (which alone vary, the true ones being always six) is fourteen, one less than in

[1] *Coup d'Œil général sur les Possessions Néerlandaises dans l'Inde Archipélagique.*

[2] TEMMINCK, *Coup d'Œil, etc.* t. i. c. iv. p. 328; t. ii. c. iii. p. 91.

the *Africanus*, *one* more than in the *Indicus*; and so it is with the dorsal vertebræ, which are twenty in the *Sumatranus* (*twenty-one* and *nineteen* in the others), whilst the new species agrees with *Africanus* in the number of sacral vertebræ (*four*), and with *Indicus* in that of the caudal ones, which are *thirty-four*." [1]

[1] *Proceed. Zool. Soc. London*, 1849, p. 144 *note*. The original description of TEMMINCK is as follows :

"Elephas Sumatranus, *Nob.* ressemble, par la forme générale du crâne, à l'éléphant du continent de l'Asie ; mais la partie libre des intermaxillaires est beaucoup plus courte et plus étroite ; les cavités nasales sont beaucoup moins larges ; l'espace entre les orbites des yeux est plus étroit ; la partie postérieure du crâne au contraire est plus large que dans l'espèce du continent.

"Les mâchelières se rapprochent, par la forme de leur couronne, plutôt de l'espèce asiatique que de celle qui est propre à l'Afrique ; c'est-à-dire que leur couronne offre la forme de rubans ondoyés et non pas en losange ; mais ces rubans sont de la largeur de ceux qu'on voit à la couronne des dents de l'éléphant d'Afrique ; ils sont conséquemment moins nombreux que dans celui du continent de l'Asie. Les dimensions de ces rubans, dans la direction d'avant en arrière, comparées à celles prises dans la direction transversale et latérale, sont en raison de 3 ou 4 à 1 ; tandis que dans l'éléphant du continent elles sont comme 4 ou 6 à 1. La longueur totale de six de ces rubans, dans l'espèce nouvelle de Sumatra, ainsi que dans celle d'Afrique, est d'environ 12 centimètres, tandis que cette longueur n'est que de 8 à 10 centimètres dans l'espèce du continent de l'Asie.

"Les autres formes ostéologiques sont à peu près les mêmes dans les trois espèces ; mais il y a différence dans le nombre des os dont le squelette se compose, ainsi que le tableau comparatif ci-joint l'éprouve.

"L'*elephas Africanus* a 7 vertèbres du cou, 21 vert. dorsales, 3 lombaires, 4 sacrées et 26 caudales ; 21 paires de côtes, dont 6 vraies et 15 fausses. L'*elephas Indicus* a 7 vertèbres du cou, 19 dorsales, 3 lombaires, 5 sacrées et 34 caudales, 19 paires de côtes, dont 6 vraies et 3 fausses. L'*elephas Sumatranus* a 7 vertèbres du cou, 20

Professor SCHLEGEL of Leyden, in a paper lately submitted by him to the Royal Academy of Sciences of Holland, (the substance of which he obligingly communicated to me, through Baron Bentinck the Netherlands Minister at this Court), confirmed the identity of the Ceylon elephant with that found in the Lampongs of Sumatra. The osteological comparison of which TEMMINCK has given the results was, he says, conducted by himself with access to four skeletons of the latter; and the more recent opportunity of comparing a living Sumatran elephant with one from Bengal, served to establish other though minor points of divergence. The Indian species is more robust and powerful; the proboscis longer and more slender; and the extremity, (a point in which the elephant of Sumatra resembles that of Africa,) is more flattened and provided with coarser and longer hair than that of India.

Professor SCHLEGEL, adverting to the large export of elephants from Ceylon to the Indian continent, which has been carried on from time immemorial, suggests the caution with which naturalists, in investigating this question, should first satisfy themselves whether the ele-

dorsales, 3 lombaires, 4 sacrées et 34 caudales; 20 paires de côtes, dont 6 vraies et 14 fausses.

"Ces caractères ont été constatés sur trois squelettes de l'espèce nouvelle, un mâle et une femelle adultes et un jeune mâle. Nous n'avons pas encore été à même de nous procurer la dépouille de cette espèce."

phants they examine are really natives of the mainland, or whether they have been brought to it from the islands. "The extraordinary fact," he observes in his letter to me, "of the identity thus established between the elephants of Ceylon and Sumatra, and the points in which they are found to differ from that of Bengal, leads to the question whether all the elephants of the Asiatic continent belong to one single species; or whether these vast regions may not produce in some quarter as yet unexplored the one hitherto found only in the two islands referred to? It is highly desirable that naturalists who have the means and opportunity, should exert themselves to discover, whether any traces are to be found of the Ceylon elephant in the Dekkan; or of that of Sumatra in Cochin China or Siam."

To me the establishment of a fact so conclusively confirmatory of the theory I had ventured to broach, was productive of great satisfaction. But in an essay by DR. FALCONER, since published in the *Natural History Review* for January 1863, "On the Living and Extinct Species of Elephants," he adduces reasons for questioning the accuracy of these views as to *Elephas Sumatranus*. The idea of a specific distinction between the elephants of India and Ceylon, Dr. Falconer shows to have been propounded as far back as 1834, by Mr. B. H. Hodgson, the eminent ethnologist and explorer of the zoology of Nepal; Dr. Falconer's own inspection however of the examples of both as preserved in the Museum of Leyden, not only did not lead him to accept the later conclusion of SCHLEGEL and TEMMINCK, but induced him to doubt the correctness of the statements published by the Prince of Canino, both as to the external and the osteological characters of the Indian elephant. As to the former, he declares that the differences between it and the elephant of Ceylon are so trifling, as not to exceed similar peculiarities observable between elephants taken in different regions of continental India, where an experienced mahout will tell at a glance, whether a newly captured animal was taken in the Sal forests of the North-Western Provinces, in Assam, in Silhet, Chittagong, Tipperah, or Cuttack. The osteological distinctions and the odontography, Dr. Falconer contends, are insufficient to sustain the alleged separateness of species. He equally discredits the alleged differences regarding the ribs and dorsal vertebræ, and he concludes that, "on a review of the whole case, the evidence in every aspect appears to him to fail in showing that the elephant of Ceylon and Sumatra is of a species distinct from that of continental India."[1] He thinks it right, however, to add, that the subject is one which "should be thoroughly investigated," as the hasty assumption that the elephants of Ceylon and Sumatra belong to distinct species has been put forward

[1] *The Natural History Review*, January 1863, pp. 81, 96.

to support the conjecture of a geological formation for the island of Ceylon distinct from that of the mainland of India; a proposition to which Dr. Falconer is not prepared to accede.

Having ventured to originate the latter theory, and having sustained it by Schlegel's authority as regards the elephant of Sumatra, I think it is incumbent on me to give becoming prominence to the opposite view entertained by one so eminently entitled to consideration as Dr. Falconer.

In the course of my observations on the structure and functions of the elephant, I have ventured an opinion that an animal of such ponderous and peculiar construction, is formed chiefly for progression by easy and steady paces, and is too weighty and unwieldy to leap, at least to any considerable height or distance. But this opinion I felt bound to advance with reserve, as I had seen in an interesting article in the *Colombo Observer* for March 1866, descriptive of a recent corral, the statement that an infuriated elephant had "fairly leaped a barrier 15 feet high, only carrying away the upper cross-beam with a crash." (See p. 40.) Doubtful of some inaccuracy in the measurements, I took the precaution of writing to Mr. Ferguson, the editor, to solicit further enquiry. Since the following pages have been printed, I have received from that gentleman the correction, which I now subjoin.

"My dear Sir Emerson,—I have just had a letter from Mr. Samuel Jayetileke, the Cutchery Modliar of Kornegalle, in reply to my queries about the height of the fence over which the elephant sprang. The result is the usual one whenever exact measurements are substituted for guess-work. I stated 15 feet as the height of the fence, and this was the information given to me at the time. But the report of Kumbowattewene, the Ratemahat-meya who has since gone to measure the place, is, that where the elephant leaped over, the height was 12 feet. The exact height of the leap was however only 9 feet; for besides that in his rush he knocked away the top bar, it is found that in the corner at which he escaped, there is a mound formed by a white ant's nest, two and a half feet high, on which he must have climbed to help him over. I trust this information may be in time to prevent my original statement from going forth without modification in your new book. The leap is still a pretty good one.—Yours faithfully, A. M. FERGUSON, *Observer Office*, Colombo, December 14, 1866."

J. EMERSON TENNENT.

TEMPO MANOR, ENNISKILLEN:
October 1, 1866.

CONTENTS.

PART I.

HABITS IN A STATE OF NATURE.

CHAPTER I.

STRUCTURE AND FUNCTIONS.

	PAGE
Vast numbers in Ceylon	4
Derivation of the word "elephant," *note*	*ib.*
Antiquity of the trade in elephants	5
Numbers now diminishing	*ib.*
Mischief done by them to crops	*ib.*
Ivory scarce in Ceylon	6
Conjectures as to the absence of tusks	7
Elephant a harmless animal	9
Alleged antipathies to other animals	11
Fights with each other	15
The foot its chief weapon	16
Use of the tusks in a wild state doubtful	17
Anecdote of sagacity in an elephant at Kandy	19
Difference between African and Indian species	20
Native ideas of perfection in an elephant	21
Blotches on the skin	22
White elephants not unknown in Ceylon	23

CHAPTER II.

HABITS WHEN WILD.

Water, but not heat, essential to elephants	25
Sight limited	26
Caution	26
Smell acute	27
Hearing good	*ib.*

	PAGE
Cries of the elephant	27
Trumpeting	28
Booming noise	29
Height, exaggerated	30
Facility of stealthy motion	31
Ancient delusion as to the joints of the leg	32
Its exposure by Sir Thos. Browne	*ib.*
Its perpetuation by poets and others	35
Position of the elephant in sleep	38
An elephant killed on its feet	39
Mode of lying down	40
Its gait a shuffle	*ib.*
Power of climbing mountains	41
Facilitated by the joint of the knee	43
Mode of descending declivities, *note*	*ib.*
A "herd" is a family	45
Attachment to their young	46
Suckled indifferently by the females	*ib.*
A "rogue" elephant	47
Their cunning and vice	48
Injuries done by them	49
The leader of a herd a tusker	50
Bathing and nocturnal gambols, description of a scene by Major Skinner	51
Method of swimming	55
Internal anatomy imperfectly known	56
Faculty of storing water	58
Peculiarity of the stomach	59
The food of the elephant	63
Sagacity in search of it	64
Unexplained dread of fences	65
Its spirit of inquisitiveness	67
Anecdotes illustrative of its curiosity	*ib.*
Estimate of sagacity	68
Singular conduct of a herd during thunder	*ib.*
An elephant feigning death	70
Appendix.—Narratives of natives, as to encounters with rogue elephants	71

CHAPTER III.

ELEPHANT SHOOTING.

Vast numbers shot in Ceylon	77
Revolting details of elephant killing in Africa, *note*	78
Fatal spots at which to aim	79
Structure of the bones of the head	*ib.*
Wounds which are certain to kill	80
Attitudes when surprised	83
Peculiar movements when reposing	84
Habits when attacked	85

Sagacity of native trackers . . . 86
Courage and agility of the elephants in escape . . . 87
Worthlessness of the carcass . . . 89
Note.—Singular recovery from a wound . . . 90

PART II.

MODE OF CAPTURE AND TRAINING.

CHAPTER I.

AN ELEPHANT CORRAL.

Early method of catching elephants . . . 96
Capture in pit-falls, *note* . . . *ib.*
By means of decoys . . . 97
Panickeas—their courage and address . . . *ib.*
Their sagacity in following the elephant . . . *ib.*
Mode of capture by the noose . . . 99
Mode of taming . . . 100
Method of leading the elephants to the coast . . . 101
Process of embarking them at Manaar . . . 102
Method of capturing a whole herd . . . 103
The "keddah" in Bengal described . . . 104
Process of enclosing a herd . . . *ib.*
Process of capture in Ceylon . . . 105
An elephant corral and its construction . . . 105
An elephant hunt in Ceylon, 1847 . . . 106
The town and district of Kornegalle . . . *ib.*
The rock of Aetagalla . . . 107
Forced labour of the corral in former times . . . 110
Now given voluntarily . . . 111
Form of the enclosure . . . 112
Method of securing a wild herd . . . 114
Scene when driving them into the corral . . . 116
A failure . . . *ib.*
An elephant drove by night . . . 118
Singular scene in the corral . . . 119
Excitement of the tame elephants, *note* . . . *ib.*

CHAPTER II.

THE CAPTIVE.

	PAGE
A night scene	121
Morning in the corral	ib.
Preparations for securing the captives	122
The "cooroowe," or noosers	ib.
The tame decoys	123
First captive tied up	124
Singular conduct of the wild elephants	126
Furious attempts of the herd to escape	127
Courageous conduct of the natives	128
Variety of disposition exhibited by the herd	131
Extraordinary contortions of the captives	ib.
Water withdrawn from the stomach	133
Instinct of the decoys	ib.
Conduct of the noosers	136
The young ones and their actions	137
Noosing a "rogue," and his death	138
Instinct of flies in search of carrion, *note*	139
Strange scene	140
A second herd captured	142
Their treatment of a solitary elephant	143
A magnificent female elephant	144
Her extraordinary attitudes	ib.
Wonderful contortions	145
Taking the captives out of the corral	147
Their subsequent treatment and training	148
Grandeur of the scene	ib.
Story of young pet elephant	149

CHAPTER III.

TRAINING AND CONDUCT IN CAPTIVITY.

Alleged superiority of the Indian to the African elephant—not true	150
Ditto of Ceylon elephant to Indian	152
Process of training in Ceylon	155
Allowed to bathe	156
Difference of disposition	158
Sudden death of "broken heart"	160
First employment treading clay	161
Drawing a waggon	ib.
Dragging timber	ib.
Sagacity in labour	ib.
Mode of raising stones	162

	PAGE
Strength in throwing down trees exaggerated . .	*ib.*
Piling timber . . .	163
Not uniform in habits of work	164
Lazy if not watched . .	165
Obedience to keeper from affection, not fear . .	*ib.*
Change of keeper—story of child	166
Ear for sounds and music .	167
Ur-re! note . . .	*ib.*
Endurance of pain . .	168
Docility	169
Working elephants, delicate.	170
Deaths in Government stud .	171
Diseases	172
Subject to tooth-ache . .	*ib.*
Question of the value of labour of an elephant . .	174
Food in captivity, and cost .	175
Breed in captivity . .	176
Age	177
Theory of M. Fleurens .	*ib.*
No dead elephants found .	179
Sindbad's story . . .	181
Appendix. — Passage from Ælian	183

LIST

OF

ILLUSTRATIONS.

	PAGE
View of an Elephant Corral	*Frontispiece*
Brain of the Elephant	26
The Trunk as figured in the fifteenth century	28
Bones of the Fore-leg	41
Elephant descending a Hill	44
Elephant's Well	55
Elephant's Stomach, showing the Water-cells	59
Elephant's Trachea	60
Water-cells in the Stomach of the Camel	62
Section of the Elephant's Skull	80
Ground Plan and Fence of a Corral	112
Noosing Wild Elephants	*to face* 124
Mode of tying an Elephant	126
His Struggles for Freedom	127
Impotent Fury	130
Singular Contortions of an Elephant	132
Attitudes of Captives	*to face* 134
Obstinate Resistance	135
Attitude for Defence	147
Figures of the African and Indian Elephants on Greek and Roman Coins	151
Medal of Numidia	156
Modern Hendoo	*ib.*

PART I.

STRUCTURE AND FUNCTIONS.

THE
WILD ELEPHANT.

CHAPTER I.

STRUCTURE AND FUNCTIONS.

DURING my residence in Ceylon, I had on two occasions opportunities of witnessing the operation on a grand scale, of capturing wild elephants, intended to be trained for the Government service in the establishment of the Civil Engineer and Commissioner of Roads;—and in the course of my frequent journeys through the interior of the island, I succeeded in collecting so many facts relative to the habits of these animals so interesting in a state of nature, as enable me not only to add to the information previously possessed, but to correct some of the fallacies popularly entertained regarding their disposition and instincts. These particulars I am anxious to place on record before proceeding to describe the scenes I allude to, during the progress of the elephant hunts in the district of the Seven Korles, at which I was present in 1846, and again in 1847.

With the exception of the narrow but densely inhabited belt of cultivated land, that extends along the seaborde from Chilaw on the western coast towards Tangalle on the south-east, there is no part of Ceylon in which elephants may not be said to abound; even close to the environs of the most populous localities of the interior. They frequent both the open plains and the deep forests; and their footsteps are to be seen wherever food and shade, vegetation and water,[1] allure

[1] M. AD. PICTET has availed himself of the love of the elephant for water, to found on it a solution of the long-contested question as to the etymology of the word "elephant,"—a term which, whilst it has passed into almost every dialect of the West, is scarcely to be traced in any language of Asia. The Greek ἐλέφας, to which we are immediately indebted for it, did not originally mean the animal, but, as early as the time of Homer, was applied only to its tusks, and signified *ivory*. BOCHART has sought for a Semitic origin, and seizing on the Arabic *fil*, and prefixing the article *al*, suggests *alfil*, akin to ἐλεφ; but rejecting this, BOCHART himself resorts to the Hebrew *eleph*, an "ox"—and this conjecture derives a certain degree of countenance from the fact that the Romans, when they obtained their first sight of the elephant in the army of Pyrrhus, in Lucania, called it the *Luca bos*. But the αντος is still unaccounted for; and POTT has sought to remove the difficulty by introducing the Arabic *hindi*, Indian, thus making *eleph hindi*, "*bos Indicus*." The conversion of *hindi* into αντος is an obstacle, but here the example of "tamarind" comes to aid; *tamar hindi*, the "Indian date," which in mediæval Greek forms ταμάρεντι. A theory of BENARY, that ἐλέφας might be compounded of the Arabic *al*, and *ibha*, a Sanskrit name for the elephant, is exposed to still greater etymological exception. PICTET's solution is, that in the Sanskrit epics "the King of Elephants," who has the distinction of carrying the god Indra, is called *airavata* or *airavana*, a modification of *airavanta*, "son of the ocean," which again comes from *iravat*, "abounding in water." "Nous aurions donc ainsi, comme corrélatif du grec ἐλέφαντα, une ancienne forme, *âirâvanta* ou *âilâvanta*, affaiblie plus tard en *âirâvata* ou *âirâvana*. . . . . On connaît la prédilection de l'éléphant pour le voisinage des fleuves, et son amour pour l'eau, dont l'abondance est nécessaire à son bien-être." This Sanskrit name, PICTET supposes, may have been carried to the West by the Phœnicians, who were the purveyors of ivory from India; and, from the Greek, the Latins derived *elephas*, which passed into the modern languages of Italy, Germany, and France. But it is curious that the Spaniards acquired from the Moors their Arabic term for ivory, *marfil*, and the Portuguese *marfim;* and that the Scandinavians, probably from their early expeditions to the Mediterranean, adopted *fill* as their name for the elephant itself, and *fil-bein* for ivory; in Danish,

them, alike on the summits of the loftiest mountains, and on the borders of the tanks and lowland streams.

From time immemorial the Singhalese have been taught to capture and tame them, and the export of elephants from Ceylon to India has been going on without interruption from the period of the first Punic War.[1] In later times in all forests elephants were the property of the Kandyan crown; and their capture or slaughter without the royal permission was classed amongst grave offences in the criminal code.

In recent years there is reason to believe that their numbers have become considerably reduced. They have entirely disappeared from localities in which they were formerly numerous;[2] smaller herds have been taken in the periodical captures for the public service, and hunters returning from the chase report them to be growing year by year more and more scarce. In consequence of this diminution the natives in some parts of the island have even suspended the ancient practice of keeping watchers and fires by night to scare away elephants from their growing crops.[3] The opening of roads too in the hill

fils-ben. (See *Journ. Asiat.* 1843, t. xliii. p. 133.) The Spaniards of South America call the palm which produces the vegetable ivory (*Phytelephas macrocarpa*) *Palma de marfil*, and the nut itself, *marfil vegetal*.

Since the above was written Gooneratné Modliar, the Singhalese Interpreter to the Supreme Court at Colombo, has supplied me with another conjecture, that the word elephant may possibly be traced to the Singhalese name of the animal, *alia*, which means literally, "the huge one." *Alia*, he adds, is not a derivation from Sanskrit or Pali, but belongs to a dialect more ancient than either.

[1] ÆLIAN, *de Nat. Anim.* lib. xvi. c. 18; COSMAS INDICOPL. p. 128.

[2] LE BRUN, who visited Ceylon A. D. 1705, says that in the district round Colombo, where elephants are now never seen, they were then so abundant, that 160 had been taken in a single corral. (*Voyage, etc.* tom. ii. ch. lxiii. p. 331.)

[3] In some parts of Bengal, where elephants were formerly troublesom

districts, and the clearing of the mountain forests of Kandy for the cultivation of coffee, have forced the animals to retire to the low country, where again they have been followed by large parties of European sportsmen; and the Singhalese themselves, being more freely provided with arms than in former times, have assisted in swelling the annual slaughter.[1]

Had the motive that incites to the destruction of the elephant in Africa and India prevailed in Ceylon, that is, had the elephants there been provided with tusks, they would long since have been annihilated for the sake of the ivory.[2] But it is a curious fact that, whilst in Africa and India both sexes have tusks,[3] with some slight

(especially near the wilds of Ramgur), the natives got rid of them by mixing a preparation of the poisonous Nepal root called *dakra* in balls of grain, and other materials, of which the animal is fond. In Cuttack, above fifty years ago, mineral poison was laid for them in the same way, and the carcases of eighty were found which had been killed thus. (*Asiat. Res.* xv. 183.)

[1] The number of elephants has been similarly reduced throughout the south of India, and as in the advancing course of enclosure and cultivation, the area within which they will be driven must become more and more contracted, the conjecture is by no means problematical, that before many generations shall have passed away, the species may become extinct in Asia.

[2] The annual importation of ivory into Great Britain alone, for the last few years, has been about *one million* pounds; which, taking the average weight of a tusk at sixty pounds, would require the slaughter of 8,333 male elephants.

But of this quantity the importation from Ceylon has generally averaged only five or six hundred weight; which, making allowance for the lightness of the tusks, would not involve the destruction of more than seven or eight in each year. At the same time, this does not fairly represent the annual number of tuskers shot in Ceylon, not only because a portion of the ivory finds its way to China and to other places, but because the chiefs and Buddhist priests have a passion for collecting tusks, and the finest and largest are to be found ornamenting their temples and private dwellings. The Chinese profess that for their exquisite carvings the ivory of Ceylon excels all other, both in density of texture and in delicacy of tint; but in the European market, the ivory of Africa, from its more distinct graining, and other causes, obtains a higher price.

[3] A writer in the *Indian Sporting Review* for October 1857 says, "In Malabar a tuskless male elephant is rare; I have seen but two." (P. 157.)

disproportion in the size of those of the females; in Ceylon, not one elephant in a hundred is found with tusks, and the few that possess them are exclusively males. Nearly all, however, have those stunted processes called *tushes*, about ten or twelve inches in length and one or two in diameter. These I have observed them to use in loosening earth, stripping off bark, and snapping asunder small branches and climbing plants; and hence tushes are seldom seen without a groove worn into them near their extremities.[1]

Amongst other surmises more ingenious than sound, the general absence of tusks in the elephant of Ceylon has been associated with the profusion of rivers and streams in the island; whilst it has been thrown out as a possibility that in Africa, where water is comparatively scarce, the animal is equipped with these implements in order to assist it in digging wells in the sand and in raising the juicy roots of the mimosas and succulent plants for the sake of their moisture. In support of this hypothesis, it has been observed, that whilst the tusks of the Ceylon species, which are never required for such uses, are slender, graceful and curved, seldom exceeding fifty or sixty pounds' weight, those of the African ele-

[1] The old fallacy is still renewed that the elephant sheds his tusks. ÆLIAN says he drops them once in ten years (lib. xiv. c. 5); and PLINY repeats the story, adding that, when dropped, the elephants hide them under ground (lib. viii.) whence SHAW says, in his *Zoology*, "they are frequently found in the woods," and exported from Africa (vol. i. p. 213); and Sir W. JARDINE in the *Naturalist's Library* (vol. ix. p. 110), says, "the tusks are shed about the twelfth or thirteenth year." This is erroneous: after losing the first pair, or, as they are called, the "milk tusks," which drop in consequence of the absorption of their roots, when the animal is extremely young, the second pair acquire their full size, and become the "permanent tusks," which are never shed.

phant are straight and thick, weighing occasionally 150 pounds, and even 300 pounds.[1] But it is manifestly inconsistent with the idea that tusks were given to the elephant to assist in digging for food, to find that the females are less bountifully supplied with them than the

[1] I have no means of ascertaining the dimensions of the largest tusks supposed to have been obtained in continental India. Of those that I have myself seen the greatest was taken from an elephant killed by Sir Victor Brooke Bart. at the Hassanoor Hills, in Coimbatore in 1863. It measured 8 feet in length, and when placed on end two men each 6 feet high can with ease stand side by side under the curved extremity. It is 1 ft. 6 in. in circumference at the base and weighs 110 lbs. This remarkable tusk is now in the museum at Colebrooke Park in the county Fermanagh. Its companion, owing to disease, is a distorted lump of ivory; an almost shapeless mass weighing 60 lbs. The life-long agony endured by the poor animal who bore it must have been frightful in the extreme. Notwithstanding the inferiority in weight of the Ceylon tusks, as compared with those of the elephant of India, it would, I think, be precipitate to draw the inference that the size of the former was uniformly and naturally less than that of the latter. The truth I believe to be, that if permitted to grow to maturity, the tusks of the one would, in all probability, equal those of the other; but, so eager is the search for ivory in Ceylon, that a tusker, when once observed in a herd, is followed up with such vigilant impatience, that he is almost invariably shot before attaining his full growth. General DE LIMA, when returning from the governorship of the Portuguese settlements at Mozambique, told me, in 1848, that he had been requested to procure two tusks of the largest size, and straightest possible shape, which were to be formed into a cross to surmount the high altar of the cathedral at Goa: he succeeded in his commission, and sent two, one of which was 180 pounds' and the other 170 pounds' weight, with the slightest possible curve. In a periodical entitled *The Friend*, published in Ceylon, it is stated in the volume for 1837 that the officers belonging to the ships Quorrah and Alburhak, engaged in the Niger Expedition, were shown by a native king two tusks, each two feet and a half in circumference at the base, eight feet long, and weighing upwards of 200 pounds. (Vol. i. p. 225.) BRODERIP, in his *Zoological Recreations*, p. 255, says a tusk of 350 pounds' weight was sold at Amsterdam, but he does not quote his authority. PETHERICK in his *Account of Egypt, Soudan*, &c. says that in Central Africa the size of tusks differs in different latitudes, those towards the north being shorter, thicker, less hollow, and heavier than those of the south. Thus a tusk from the Nouaer, Dinka, or Shilook tribes will weigh 120 lbs., while one from Bari would weigh only 70 lbs. or 80 lbs. "Indeed," he adds, "I have known a tusk from Nouaer to weigh 185 lbs., its length being *seven feet two inches*, and its greatest thickness at the base *nine* inches." (PETHERICK, p. 418.) Sir S. Baker, in his explorations of the White Nile, saw monster tusks of 160 lbs.: and one in the possession of a trader weighed 172 lbs. (*The Albert Nyanza*, vol. i. p. 273.)

males, whilst the necessity for their use extends alike to both sexes. The same consideration serves to demonstrate the fallacy of the conjecture, that the tusks of the elephant were given as weapons of offence, for if such were the case the vast majority of them in Ceylon, males as well as females, would be left helpless in presence of an assailant. But although in their conflicts with one another, those which are provided with tusks may occasionally push clumsily with them at an opponent, it is a misapprehension to imagine that tusks are designed, as has been stated, to serve "in warding off the attacks of the wily tiger and the furious rhinoceros, often securing the victory by one blow which transfixes the assailant to the earth." [1]

So peaceable and harmless is the life of the elephant, that nature appears to have left it unprovided with any special weapon of offence: the trunk is too delicate an organ to be rudely employed in a conflict with other animals, and although on an emergency it may push or gore with its tusks (to which the French have hastily given the designation of "*défenses*"), their almost vertical position, added to the difficulty of raising its head above the level of the shoulder, is inconsistent with the idea of their being designed for attack, since it is impossible for the animal to deliver an effectual blow, or to

[1] *Menageries, etc.* published by the Society for the Diffusion of Useful Knowledge, vol. i. p. 68: "The Elephant," ch. iii. It will be seen that I have quoted repeatedly from this volume, because it is the most compendious and careful compilation with which I am acquainted of the information previously existing regarding the elephant. The author incorporates no speculations of his own, but has most diligently and agreeably arranged all the facts collected by his predecessors. The story of antipathy between the elephant and rhinoceros is probably borrowed from ÆLIAN *de Nat.* lib. xvii. c. 44.

"wield" its tusks as the deer and the buffalo can wield their horns.[1] Nor is it easy to conceive under what circumstances an elephant could have a hostile encounter with a rhinoceros or a tiger, since their respective pursuits in a state of nature can in no way conflict.

Towards man the elephant evinces shyness, arising from love of solitude and dislike of intrusion ; any alarm exhibited at his appearance may be reasonably traced to the slaughter which has reduced their numbers ; and as some evidence of this, it has always been observed in Ceylon that an elephant manifests greater impatience of the presence of a white man than of a native. Were its instincts to carry it further, or were it influenced by any feeling of animosity or malignity, it must be apparent that, as against the prodigious numbers that inhabit the forests of the island, man would wage an unequal contest, and that of the two, one or other must long since have been reduced to a helpless minority.

Official testimony is not wanting in confirmation of this view : in the returns of 108 coroner's inquests in Ceylon, during five years from 1849 to 1855 inclusive, held in cases of death occasioned by wild animals, 15 are recorded as having been caused by buffaloes, 6 by croco-

[1] "The *Correspondencia* of Madrid gives the following account of a fight between a Ceylon elephant and two bulls, which took place at Saragossa :—'The elephant was walking quietly about the arena when the first bull was released and rushed at it with all his might. The elephant received his antagonist with great coolness, and threw him down with the utmost ease. The bull rose again and made two more attacks, which the elephant resented by killing him with his tusks. The conqueror did not seem in the least excited, but quietly drank some water offered by his keeper, and ate several ears of Indian corn. A second bull was then released, and in a few minutes suffered the same fate as the first.'" (*Globe*, Nov. 9, 1864.) The *Times* says the elephant killed it "*with a thrust* of his tusks."

diles, 2 by boars, 1 by a bear, and 68 by serpents (the great majority of the last class of sufferers being women and children, who had been bitten during the night), and 16 by elephants. Little more than three fatal accidents occurring annually on the average of five years, is certainly a very small proportion in a population estimated at a million and a half, in an island abounding with wild elephants, with which, independently of casual encounters, voluntary conflicts are daily stimulated by the love of sport or the hope of gain. Were the elephants instinctively vicious or even highly irritable in their temperament, the destruction of human life under the circumstances must have been infinitely greater. It must also be taken into account, that some of the accidents recorded may have occurred in the rutting season, when even tame elephants are subject to fits of temporary fury, known in India by the term *must*, in Ceylon *mudda*,—a paroxysm which speedily passes away, but during the fury of which it is dangerous even for the mahout who has charge of them to approach those ordinarily the gentlest and most familiar.

Again, the elephant is said to "entertain an extraordinary dislike to all quadrupeds; that dogs running near it produce annoyance; that it is alarmed if a hare start from her form;" and from Pliny to Buffon every naturalist has asserted its supposed aversion to swine.[1] These

[1] *Menageries, etc.*: "The Elephant," ch. iii. In the Anglo-Saxon *Epistola Alexandri ad Aristotelem*, which has been printed by COCKAYNE in his *Narratiuncvlæ Anglice conscriptæ*, the belief in the alleged antipathy of the elephant to swine is embodied in the text and is thus rendered in the Latin version: "Pervenimus demum ad silvas Indorum ultimas; ubi cum castra collocavissemus, ceperamus velle epulari sub nocte hora xi; cum subito pabulatores

alleged antipathies are in a great degree, if not altogether, imaginary. The habits of the elephant are essentially harmless, its wants lead to no rivalry with other animals, and the food to which it is most attached flourishes in such luxuriance that abundance of it is obtained without an effort. In the quiet solitudes of Ceylon, elephants may be seen browsing peacefully in the immediate vicinity of other animals, and often in close contact with them. I have seen groups of deer and wild buffaloes reclining in the sandy bed of a river in the dry season, and elephants plucking the branches above and beside them. They show no impatience in the company of the elk, the bear, and the wild hog; and on the other hand, I have never discovered an instance in which these animals have evinced any apprehension of the elephant. Its natural timidity, however, is such that it becomes alarmed on the appearance in the jungle of any animal with whose form it is not familiar. It is said to be afraid of the horse; but from my own experience, I should say it is the horse that is disquieted at the aspect of the elephant. In the same way, from some unaccountable impulse, the

lignatoresque exanimes nunciabant, ut celeriter arma caperemus, venire e silvis elephantorum immensas greges ad expugnanda castra.' Imperavi ergo Thessalicis equitibus ut ascenderent equos, *secumque tollerent sucs*, quorum grunnitus timere bestias noveram, et occurrere quam primum elephantis jussi . . . . . . nec mora trepidantes elephanti conversi sunt. Quieta nox fuit usque ad lucem." (P. 58.) Another allusion to the same legendary incident will be found in the *Lyfe of Alisaunder*, one of the most ancient English romances, reprinted by WEBER in his *Metrical Romances of the 13th, 14th, and 15th Centuries.*

"Forth went the kyng thennes with hy;
Of the forme-ward he herd grete cry
For hy weren assailed of olifauntz.
The kyng highed, and his sergeauntz:
Ac, so I fynde on the booke,
By Porus conseil *hogges hy took*
And beten them so they shrightte:
The olifauntz away hem dightte;
For hy ne have so mychel drade
Of nothing as of hogges grade."

WEBER, vol. i. p. 237.

horse has an antipathy to the camel, and evinces extreme impatience, both of the sight and the smell of that animal.[1] When enraged, an elephant will not hesitate to charge a rider on horseback; but it is against the man, not against the horse, that his fury is directed; and no instance has been ever known of his wantonly assailing a horse. A horse belonging to the late Major Rogers[2] had run away from his groom, and was found some considerable time afterwards grazing quietly with a herd of elephants. In DE BRY's splendid collection of travels, however, there is included *The voyage of a certain Englishman to Cambay;* in which the author asserts that at Agra, in the year 1607, he was present at a spectacle given by the viceregent of the great Mogul, in the course of which he saw an elephant destroy two horses, by seizing them in its trunk, and crushing them with his tusks and feet.[3] But this display was avowedly an artificial one, and the creature must have been cruelly trained and tutored for the occasion.

[1] This peculiarity was noticed by the ancients, and is recorded by Herodotus: κάμηλον ἵππος φοβέεται, καὶ οὐκ ἀνέχεται οὔτε τὴν ἰδέην αὐτῆς ὁρέων οὔτε τὴν ὀδμὴν ὀσφραινόμενος. (Herod. ch. 80.) Camels have long been bred by the Grand Duke of Tuscany, at his establishment near Pisa, and even there the same instinctive dislike to them is manifested by the horse, which it is necessary to train and accustom to their presence in order to avoid accidents. Mr. BRODERIP mentions, that, "when the precaution of such training has not been adopted, the sudden and dangerous terror with which a horse is seized in coming unexpectedly upon one of them is excessive."—*Note-book of a Naturalist*, ch. iv. p. 113.

[2] Major ROGERS was many years the chief civil officer of the Ceylon Government in the district of Ouvah, where he was killed by lightning, 1845.

[3] "Quidam etiam cum equis silvestribus pugnant. Sæpe unus elephas cum sex equis committitur; atque ipse adeo interfui cum unus elephas duos equos cum primo impetu protinus prosternerit;—injecta enim jugulis ipsorum longa proboscide, ad se protractos, dentibus porro comminuit ac protrivit." (*Angli cujusdam in Cambayam navigatio.* DE BRY, *Coll. etc.* vol. iii. ch. xvi. p. 31.)

Pigs are constantly to be seen feeding about the stables of tame elephants, which manifest no repugnance to them. As to smaller animals, the elephant undoubtedly evinces uneasiness at the presence of a dog, but this is referable to the same cause as its impatience of a horse, namely, that neither is habitually seen by it in the forest; and it would be idle to suppose that this feeling could amount to hostility against a creature incapable of inflicting on it the slightest injury.[1] The truth I apprehend to be that, when they meet, the impudence and impertinences of the dog are offensive to the gravity of the elephant, and incompatible with his love of solitude and noiseless repose. Or, as regards the horse and the dog, may it be assumed as an evidence of the sagacity of the elephant, that the only two animals to which it manifests an antipathy, are the two which it has seen only in the company of its greatest enemy, man? One instance has certainly been attested to me by an eye-witness, in which the trunk of an elephant was seized in the teeth of a Scotch terrier, and such was the alarm of the huge creature that it came at once to its knees. The dog repeated the attack, and on every renewal of it the elephant retreated in terror, holding its trunk above its head, and kicking at the terrier with its fore feet. It would have turned to flight but for the interference of its keeper.

[1] To account for the impatience manifested by the elephant at the presence of a dog, it has been suggested that he is alarmed lest the latter should attack *his feet*, a portion of his body of which the elephant is peculiarly careful. A tame elephant has been observed to regard with indifference a spear directed towards his head, but to shrink timidly from the same weapon when pointed at his feet.

Major Skinner, formerly commissioner of roads in Ceylon, whose official duties in constructing highways involved the necessity of his being in the jungle for months together, always found that, by night or by day, the barking of a dog which accompanied him was sufficient to put a herd of wild elephants to flight. On the whole, therefore, I am of opinion that in a state of nature the elephant lives on terms of amity with every animal in the forest, that it neither regards them as its foes, nor provokes their hostility by its acts; and that, with the exception of man, its greatest enemy is a fly!

These current statements as to the supposed animosity of the elephant to minor animals originated with Ælian and Pliny, who had probably an opportunity of seeing, what may at any time be observed, that when a captive elephant is picketed beside a post, the domestic animals, goats, sheep, and cattle, will annoy and irritate it by their audacity in making free with its provender; but this is an evidence in itself of the little instinctive dread which such comparatively puny creatures entertain of one so powerful and yet so gentle.

Amongst elephants themselves, jealousy and other causes of irritation frequently occasion contentions between individuals of the same herd; but on such occasions their general habit is to strike with their trunks, and to bear down their opponents with their heads. It is doubtless correct that an elephant, when prostrated by the force and fury of an antagonist of its own species, is often wounded by the downward pressure of the tusks, which in any other position it would be almost impossible to use offensively.[1]

Mr. Mercer, who in 1846 was the principal civil officer of Government at Badulla, sent me a jagged fragment of an elephant's tusk, about five inches in diameter, and weighing between twenty and thirty pounds, which had been brought to him by some natives, who, being attracted by a noise in the jungle, witnessed a combat between a tusker and one without tusks, and saw the latter with his trunk seize one of the tusks of his antagonist and wrench from it the portion in question, which measured two feet in length.

Here the trunk was shown to be the more powerful offensive weapon of the two; but I apprehend that the chief reliance of the elephant for defence is on its ponderous weight, the pressure of its foot being sufficient to crush any minor assailant after being prostrated by means of its trunk. Besides, in using its feet for this purpose, it derives a wonderful facility from the peculiar formation of the knee-joint in the hind leg, which, enabling it to swing the hind feet forward close to the ground, assists it to toss the body alternately from foot to foot, till deprived of life.[2]

[1] A writer in the *Indian Sporting Review* for October 1857 says a male elephant was killed by two others close to his camp: "the head was completely smashed in; there was a large hole in the side, and the abdomen was ripped open. The latter wound was given probably after it had fallen." (P. 175.)

[2] In the Third Book of Maccabees, which is not printed in our Apocrypha, but appears in the series in the Greek Septuagint, the author, in describing the persecution of the Jews by Ptolemy Philopater, B.C. 210, states that the king swore vehemently that he would send them into the other world, "foully trampled to death by the knees and feet of elephants" (πέμψειν εἰς ᾅδην ἐν γόνασι καὶ ποσὶ θηρίων ᾐκισμένους. 3 Mac. v. 42). ÆLIAN makes the remark, that elephants on such occasions use their *knees* as well as their feet to crush their victim. (*Hist. Anim.* viii. 10.)

A sportsman who had partially undergone this operation, having been seized by a wounded elephant but escaped from its fury, described to me his sufferings as he was thus flung back and forward between the hind and fore feet of the animal, which ineffectually attempted to trample him at each concussion, and abandoned him without inflicting serious injury.

KNOX, in describing the execution of criminals by the state elephants of the former kings of Kandy, says, "they will run their teeth (*tusks*) through the body, and then tear it in pieces and throw it limb from limb;" but a Kandyan chief, who was witness to these scenes, assured me that the elephant never once applied its tusks, but, placing its foot on the prostrate victim, plucked off his limbs in succession by a sudden movement of the trunk. If the tusks were designed to be employed offensively, some alertness would naturally be exhibited in using them; but in numerous instances where sportsmen have fallen into the power of a wounded elephant, they have escaped through the failure of the enraged animal to strike them with its tusks, even when stretched upon the ground.[1]

But here there arises a further and a very curious enquiry, as to the specific objects in the economy of the elephant, to which its tusks are conducive. Placed as it is in Ceylon, in the midst of the most luxuriant profusion of its favourite food, in close proximity at all times to abundant supplies of water, and with no natural enemies against whom to protect itself, it is difficult to

[1] The *Hastisilpe*, a Singhalese work which treats of the "Science of Elephants," enumerates amongst those which it is not desirable to possess, "the elephant which will fight with a stone or a stick in his trunk."

conjecture any probable utility which it can derive from such appendages. Their absence is unaccompanied by any inconvenience to the individuals in whom they are wanting; and as regards the few who possess them, the only operations in which I am aware of their tusks being employed in relation to the habits of the animal, is to assist in ripping open the stem of the jaggery palms and young palmyras to extract the farinaceous core; and in splitting up the juicy shaft of the plantain. Whilst the tuskless elephant crushes the latter under foot, thereby soiling it and wasting its moisture; the other, by opening it with the point of its tusk, performs the operation with delicacy and apparent ease.

These, however, are trivial and almost accidental advantages: on the other hand, owing to irregularities in their growth, the tusks are sometimes an impediment to the animal in feeding;[1] and in more than one instance in the Government studs, tusks which had so grown as to approach and cross one another at the extremities, have had to be relieved by the saw; the contraction of space between them so impeding the free action of the trunk as to prevent the animal from conveying branches to its mouth.[2]

It is true that in captivity, and after a due course of

[1] Among other eccentric forms, an elephant was seen in 1844, in the district of Bintenne, near Friar's-Hood Mountain, one of whose tusks was so bent that it took what sailors term a "round turn," and then resumed its curved direction as before. In the Museum of the College of Surgeons, London, there is a specimen, No. 2757, of a *spiral* tusk.

[2] Since the foregoing remarks were written relative to the undefined use of tusks to the elephant, I have seen a speculation on the same subject in Dr. Holland's "*Constitution of the Animal Creation, as expressed in structural appendages;*" but the conjecture of the author leaves the problem scarcely less obscure than before. Struck with the mere *supplemental*

training, the elephant discovers a new use for its tusks when employed in moving stones and piling timber; so much so that a powerful one will raise and carry on them a log of half a ton weight or more. One evening, whilst riding in the vicinity of Kandy, towards the scene of the massacre of Major Davie's party in 1803, my horse evinced some excitement at a noise which approached us in the thick jungle, and which consisted of a repetition of the ejaculation *urmph! urmph!* in a hoarse and dissatisfied tone. A turn in the forest explained the mystery, by bringing me face to face with a tame elephant, unaccompanied by any attendant. He was labouring painfully to carry a heavy beam of timber, which he balanced across his tusks, but the pathway being narrow, he was forced to bend his head to one side to permit the load to pass endways; and the exertion and this inconvenience combined led him to utter the dissatisfied sounds which disturbed the composure of my horse. On seeing us halt, the elephant raised his head, reconnoitred us for a moment, then flung down the timber, and voluntarily forced himself backwards among the brushwood so as to leave a passage, of which he expected us to avail ourselves. My horse hesitated: the elephant observed it, and impatiently thrust himself still

presence of the tusks, the absence of all apparent use serving to distinguish them from the *essential* organs of the creature, Dr. HOLLAND concludes that their production is a process incident, but not ancillary, to other important ends, especially connected with the vita functions of the trunk and the marvellous motive powers inherent to it; his conjecture is, that they are "a species of safety valve of the animal œconomy,"—and that "they owe their development to the predominance of the senses of touch and smell, conjointly with the muscular motions of which the exercise of these is accompanied." "Had there been no proboscis," he thinks, "there would have been no supplementary appendages,—the former creates the latter." (Pp. 246, 271.)

deeper into the jungle, repeating his cry of *urmph!* but in a voice evidently meant to encourage us to advance. Still the horse trembled; and anxious to observe the instinct of the two sagacious animals, I laid the rein upon its neck and forbore any interference: again the elephant of his own accord wedged himself further in amongst the trees, and manifested some impatience that we did not pass him. At length the horse moved forward; and when we were fairly past the elephant I looked back and saw the wise creature stoop and take up its unwieldy burthen, trim and balance it on its tusks, and resume its route as before, hoarsely snorting its discontented remonstrance.

Between the African elephant and that of Ceylon, with the exception of the striking peculiarity of the infrequency of tusks in the latter, the distinctions are less apparent to a casual observer than to a scientific naturalist. In the Ceylon species the forehead is higher and more hollow, the ears are smaller, and, in a section of the teeth, the grinding ridges, instead of being lozenge-shaped, are transverse bars of uniform breadth.

The Indian elephant is stated by Cuvier to have four nails on the hind foot, the African variety having only three; but amongst the perfections of a high-bred elephant of Ceylon, is always enumerated the possession of *twenty* nails, whilst those of a secondary class have but eighteen in all.[1]

[1] See *Notes on the Natural History of Ceylon* by Sir J. EMERSON TENNENT, p. 60. Sir S. BAKER adds as a distinctive feature of the African elephant that its "back is concave while that of the Indian variety is convex." (*The Albert Nyanza*, vol. i. p. 274.)

So conversant are the natives with the structure and "points" of the elephant, that they divide them readily into castes, and describe with particularity their distinctive excellences and defects. In the *Hastisilpe*, a Singhalese work which treats of their natural management, the marks of inferior breeding are said to be "eyes restless like those of a crow, the hair of the head of mixed shades; the face wrinkled; the tongue curved and black; the nails short and green; the ears small; the neck thin, the skin freckled; the tail without a tuft, and the fore-quarter lean and low;" whilst the perfection of form and beauty is supposed to consist in the "softness of the skin, the red colour of the mouth and tongue, the forehead expanded and hollow, the ears broad and rectangular, the trunk broad at the root and blotched with pink in front; the eyes bright and kindly, the cheeks large, the neck full, the back level, the chest square, the fore legs short and convex in front, the hind quarter plump, and five nails on each foot, all smooth, polished, and round.[1] An elephant with these perfections," says the author of the *Hastisilpe*, "will impart glory and magnificence to the king; but he cannot be discovered amongst thousands, yea, there shall never be found an elephant clothed at once with *all* the excellences herein described." The "points" of an elephant are to be studied with the greatest advantage in those attached to the temples, which are always of the highest caste, and exhibit the most perfect breeding.

[1] A native of rank informed me, that "the tail of a high-caste elephant will sometimes touch the ground, but such are very rare."

The colour of the animal's skin in a state of nature is generally of a lighter brown than that of those in captivity; a distinction which arises, in all probability, not so much from the wild animal's propensity to cover itself with mud and dust, as from the superior care which is taken in repeatedly bathing the tame ones, and in rubbing their skins with a soft stone, a lump of burnt clay, or the rough husk of a coco-nut. This kind of discipline, together with the occasional application of oil, gives rise to the deeper black which the hides of the latter present.

Amongst the Singhalese, however, a singular preference is evinced for elephants that exhibit those flesh-coloured blotches which occasionally mottle the skin of an elephant, chiefly about the head and extremities. The front of the trunk, the tips of the ears, the forehead, and occasionally the legs, are thus diversified with stains of a yellowish tint, inclining to pink. These are not natural; nor are they hereditary, for they are seldom exhibited by the younger individuals in a herd, but appear to be the result of some eruptive affection, the irritation of which has induced the animal in its uneasiness to rub itself against the rough bark of trees, and thus to abrade the outer cuticle.[1]

To a European these spots appear blemishes, and the taste that leads the natives to admire them is probably akin to the feeling that has at all times rendered *a white*

[1] This is confirmed by the fact that the scar of the ancle wound, occasioned by the rope on the legs of those which have been captured by noosing, presents precisely the same tint when thoroughly healed.

elephant an object of wonder to Asiatics. The rarity of the latter is accounted for by regarding this peculiar appearance as the result of albinism; and notwithstanding the exaggeration of Oriental historians, who compare the fairness of such creatures to the whiteness of snow, even in its utmost perfection, I apprehend that the tint of a white elephant is little else than a flesh-colour, rendered somewhat more conspicuous by the blanching of the skin, and the lightness of the colourless hairs with which it is sparsely covered. A white elephant is mentioned in the *Mahawanso* as forming part of the retinue attached to the "Temple of the Tooth" at Anarajapoora, in the fifth century after Christ;[1] but it commanded no religious veneration, and like those in the stud of the kings of Siam, it was tended merely as an emblem of royalty;[2] the sovereign of Ceylon being addressed as the "Lord of Elephants."[3] At the same time it admits of no doubt that in the early ages, white animals were in some parts of the East the objects of devout adoration. Herodotus alludes to the sacred white horses, *ἱερῶν ἵππων τῶν λευκῶν*, which accompanied the army of Cyrus to the siege of Babylon;[4] he equally records that amongst the Egyptians purely white oxen were sacred to Epaphus; but one single dark hair was enough to exclude them as unclean.[5]

In 1633 a white elephant was exhibited in Holland;[6]

[1] *Mahawanso*, ch. xxxviii. p. 254, A.D. 433.

[2] PALLEGOIX, *Siam, etc.* vol. i. p. 152.

[3] *Mahawanso*, ch. xviii. p. 111. The Hindu sovereigns of Orissa, in the middle ages, bore the style of *Gajapati*, "powerful in elephants." (*Asiat. Res.* xv. 253.)

[4] Herod. l. i. c. 189.

[5] Ibid. l. ii. c. 38.

[6] ARMANDI, *Hist. Milit. des Elé-*

but as this was some years before the Dutch had established themselves firmly in Ceylon, it was probably brought from some other of their eastern possessions.

phants, lib. ii. c. x. p. 380. HORACE mentions a white elephant as having been exhibited at Rome: "Sive elephas albus vulgi converteret ora." (HOR. *Ep.* II. 196.)

CHAPTER II.

HABITS WHEN WILD.

ALTHOUGH found generally in warm and sunny climates, it is a mistake to suppose that the elephant is partial either to heat or to light. In Ceylon, the mountain tops, and not the sultry valleys, are its favourite resort. In Ouvah, where the elevated plains are often crisp with the morning frost, and on Pedura-talla-galla, at the height of upwards of eight thousand feet, they may be found in herds at times when the hunter will search for them without success in the hot jungles of the low country. No altitude, in fact, seems too lofty or too chill for the elephant, provided it affords the luxury of water in abundance; and, contrary to the general opinion that the elephant delights in sunshine, it seems at all times impatient of glare, and spends the day in the thickest depth of the forests, devoting the night to excursions, and to the luxury of the bath, in which it also indulges occasionally by day. This partiality for shade is doubtless ascribable to the animal's love of coolness and solitude; but it is not altogether unconnected with the position of the eye, and the circumscribed use which its peculiar mode of life permits it to make of the faculty of sight.

All the elephant hunters and natives with whom I have spoken on the subject, concur in opinion that its range of vision is circumscribed, and that it relies more on the ear and the sense of smell than on its sight, which is liable to be obstructed by dense foliage; besides which, from the formation of its short neck, the elephant is incapable of directing the range of the eye much above the level of the head.[1]

This small sphere of vision is sufficient to account for the excessive caution of the elephant, its alarm at unusual

[1] After writing the above, I was permitted by the late Dr. HARRISON, of Dublin, to see some accurate drawings of the brain of an elephant, which he had the opportunity of dissecting in 1847; and on looking to that of the base, I have found a remarkable verification of the information which I had previously collected in Ceylon.

The small figure A is the ganglion of the fifth nerve, showing the small motor and large sensitive portion.

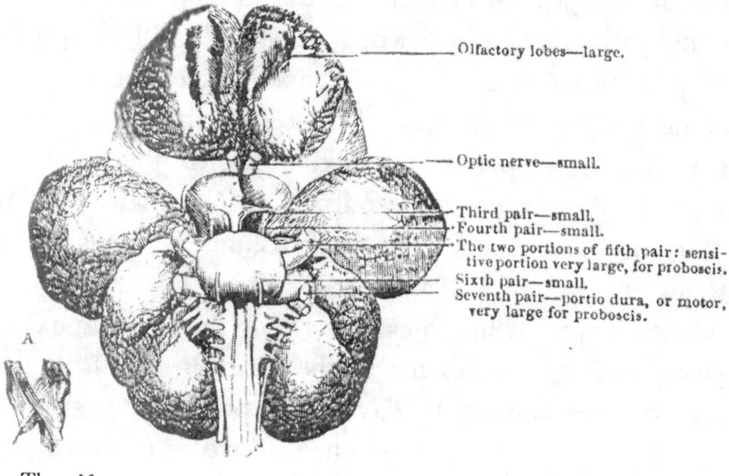

The *olfactory lobes*, from which the olfactory nerves proceed, are large, whilst the *optic and muscular nerves of the orbit are singularly small* for so vast an animal; and one is immediately struck by the prodigious size of the fifth nerve, which supplies the proboscis with its exquisite sensibility, as well as by the great size of the motor portion of the seventh, which supplies the same organ with its power of movement and action.

noises, and the timidity and panic exhibited at trivial objects and incidents which, imperfectly discerned, excite suspicions for its safety.[1] In 1841 an officer[2] was chased by an elephant that he had slightly wounded. Seizing him near the dry bed of a river, the animal had its fore-foot already raised to crush him; but its forehead being touched at the same instant by the tendrils of a climbing plant which had suspended itself from the branches above, it suddenly turned and fled; leaving him badly hurt, but with no limb broken. I have heard similar instances, equally well attested, of this peculiarity in the character of the elephant.

On the other hand, the power of smell is so remarkable as almost to compensate for the deficiency of sight. A herd is not only apprised of the approach of danger by this means, but when scattered in the forest, and dispersed out of range of sight, they are enabled by it to reassemble with rapidity and to adopt precautions for their common safety. The same necessity is met by a delicate sense of hearing, and the use of a variety of noises or calls, by means of which elephants succeed in communicating with each other upon all emergencies. "The sounds which they utter have been described by the African hunters as of three kinds: the first, which is very shrill, produced by blowing through the trunk, is indicative of pleasure; the second, produced by the mouth, is expressive of want; and the third, proceeding

[1] *Menageries, etc.* "The Elephant," p. 27.

[2] Major Rogers. An account of this singular adventure will be found in the *Ceylon Miscellany* for 1842, vol. i. p. 221.

from the throat, is a terrific roar of anger or revenge."[1] These words convey but an imperfect idea of the variety of noises made by the elephant in Ceylon; and the shrill cry produced by blowing through his trunk, so far from being regarded as an indication of "pleasure," is the well-known cry of rage with which he rushes to encounter an assailant. ARISTOTLE describes it as resembling the hoarse sound of a "trumpet."[2] The French still designate the proboscis of an elephant by the same expression "trompe" (which we have unmeaningly corrupted into *trunk*), and hence the scream of the elephant

[1] *Menageries, etc.* "The Elephant," ch. iii. p. 68.

[2] ARISTOTLE, *De Anim.* lib. iv. c. 9, ὁμοῖον σάλπιγγι. See also PLINY, lib. x. ch. cxiii. A manuscript of the 15th century in the British Museum, containing the romance of "*Alexander*," which is probably of the fifteenth century, is interspersed with drawings illustrative of the strange animals of the East. Amongst them are two elephants, whose trunks are literally in the form of *trumpets with expanded mouths.* See WRIGHT'S *Archæological Album*, p. 176, and M.S. Reg. 15, e, vi. Brit. Mus.

is known as "trumpeting" by the hunters in Ceylon. Their cry when in pain, or when subjected to compulsion, is a grunt or a deep groan from the throat, with the proboscis curled upwards and the lips wide apart.

Should the attention of an individual in the herd be attracted by any unusual appearance in the forest, the intelligence is rapidly communicated by a low suppressed sound made by the lips, somewhat resembling the twittering of a bird, and described by the hunters by the word "*prut.*"

A very remarkable noise has been described to me by more than one individual, who had come unexpectedly upon a herd during the night, when the alarm of the elephants was apparently too great to be satisfied with the stealthy note of warning just described. On these occasions the sound produced resembled the hollow booming of an empty tun when struck with a wooden mallet or a muffled sledge. Major MACREADY, Military Secretary in Ceylon in 1836, who heard it by night amongst the wild elephants in the great forest of Bintenne, describes it as "a sort of banging noise like that of a cooper hammering a cask;" and Major SKINNER is of opinion that it must be produced by the elephant striking his ribs rapidly and forcibly with his trunk. Mr. CRIPPS informs me that he has more than once seen an elephant, when surprised or alarmed, produce this sound by beating the ground forcibly with the flat side of the trunk; and this movement was instantly succeeded by raising it again, and pointing it in the direction whence the alarm proceeded, as if to ascertain by the sense of smell the nature of the threatened danger. As this strange sound is generally mingled with the bellowing and ordinary trumpeting of the herd, it is in all probability a device resorted to, not alone for warning their companions of some approaching peril, but also for the additional purpose of terrifying unseen intruders.[1]

Elephants are subject to deafness; and the Singhalese regard as the most formidable of all wild animals, a "rogue"[2] afflicted with this infirmity.

Extravagant estimates are recorded of the height of the elephant. In an age when popular fallacies in relation to him were as yet uncorrected in Europe by the actual inspection of the living animal, he was supposed to grow to the height of twelve or fifteen feet. Even within the last century, in popular works on natural history, the elephant, when full grown, was said to measure from seventeen to twenty feet from the ground to the shoulder.[3] At a still later period, so imperfectly had the truth been ascertained, that the elephant of Ceylon was believed "to excel that of Africa in size and strength."[4] But so far from equalling the size of the

[1] PALLEGOIX, in his *Description du Royaume Thai ou Siam*, adverts to a sound produced by the elephant when weary: "quand il est fatigué, *il frappe la terre avec sa trompe*, et en tire un son semblable à celui du cor." (Tom. i. p. 151.)

[2] For an explanation of the term "rogue" as applied to an elephant, see p. 47.

[3] *Natural History of Animals.* By Sir JOHN HILL, M.D. London, 1748 52, p. 565. A probable source of these false estimates is mentioned by a writer in the *Indian Sporting Review* for Oct. 1857. "Elephants were measured formerly, and even now, by natives, as to their height, by throwing a rope over them, the ends brought to the ground on each side, and half the length taken as the true height. Hence the origin of elephants fifteen and sixteen feet high. A rod held at right angles to the measuring rod, and parallel to the ground, will rarely give more than ten feet, the majority being under nine." (P. 159.)

[4] SHAW's *Zoology*. Lond. 1806. vol. i. p. 216; ARMANDI, *Hist. Milit. des Eléphants*, liv. i. ch. i. p. 2.

African species, that of Ceylon seldom exceeds the height of nine feet; even in the Hambangtotte country, where the hunters agree that the largest specimens are to be found, the tallest in ordinary herds do not average more than eight feet. WOLF, in his account of the Ceylon elephant,[1] says he saw one taken near Jaffna, which measured twelve feet and one inch high. But the truth is, that the general bulk of the elephant so far exceeds that of the animals we are accustomed to see daily, that the imagination magnifies its unusual dimensions; and I have seldom or ever met with an inexperienced spectator who did not unconsciously overestimate the size of an elephant shown to him, whether in captivity or in a state of nature. Major DENHAM would have guessed some which he saw in Africa to be sixteen feet in height, but the largest when killed was found to measure nine feet six, from the foot to the hip-bone.[2]

For a creature of such extraordinary weight it is astonishing how noiselessly and stealthily the elephant

[1] WOLF'S *Life and adventures, etc.* p. 164. Wolf was a native of Mecklenburg, who arrived in Ceylon about 1750, as chaplain in one of the Dutch East Indiamen, and having been taken into the Government employment, he served for twenty years at Jaffna, first as Secretary to the Governor, and afterwards in an office the duties of which he describes to be the examination and signature of the "writings which served to commence a suit in any of the courts of justice." His book embodies a truthful and generally accurate account of the northern portion of the island, with which alone he was conversant, and his narrative gives a curious insight into the policy of the Dutch Government, and of the condition of the natives under their dominion.

[2] DENHAM'S *Travels, etc.* 4to, p. 220. Fossil remains of the Indian elephant have been discovered at Jabalpur, showing a height of fifteen feet. (*Journ. Asiat. Soc. Beng.* vi.) Professor ANSTED in his *Ancient World*, p. 197, says he was informed by Dr. Falconer "that out of eleven hundred elephants from which the tallest were selected and measured with care, on one occasion in India, there was not one whose height equalled eleven feet."

can escape from a pursuer. When suddenly disturbed in the jungle, it will burst away with a rush that seems to bear down all before it; but the noise sinks into absolute stillness so suddenly, that a novice might well be led to suppose that the fugitive had only halted within a few yards of him, when further search will disclose that it has stolen silently away, making scarcely a sound in its escape; and, stranger still, leaving the foliage almost undisturbed by its passage.

The most venerable delusion respecting the elephant, and that which held its ground with unequalled tenacity, is the ancient fallacy thus set out by Sir THOMAS BROWNE in his *Pseudodoxia Epidemica.* "The elephant, it is said, hath no joynts; and this absurdity is seconded by another, that being unable to lye downe it sleepeth against a tree, which the hunters observing doe saw almost asunder, whereon the beast relying, by the fall of the tree falls also downe it-selfe and is able to rise no more."[1] Sir THOMAS is disposed to think that "the hint and ground of this opinion might be the grosse and somewhat cylindricall composure of the legs of the elephant, and the equality and lesse perceptible disposure of the joynts, especially in the forelegs of this animal, they appearing, when he standeth, like pillars of flesh;" but he overlooks the fact that PLINY has ascribed the same peculiarity to the Scandinavian beast somewhat resembling

[1] *Vulgar Errors*, book iii. chap. 1. The earliest English writer who promulgated this error was ALEXANDER NECKHAM, who in his treatise *De Naturis Rerum*, composed in the 12th century, quotes Cassiodorus and accepts his assertion that the elephant has no joints, chap. cxliii. NECKHAM repeats the statement in his poem *De Laudibus Divinæ Sapientiæ*, v. 47.

a horse, which he calls a "machlis,"[1] and that CÆSAR in describing the wild animals in the Hercynian forests, enumerates the *alce* (elk?), "in colour and configuration approaching the goat, but surpassing it in size, its head destitute of horns *and its limbs of joints*, whence it can neither lie down to rest, nor rise if by any accident it should fall, but using the trees for a resting-place, the hunters by loosening their roots bring the *alce* to the ground, so soon as it is tempted to lean on them."[2] This fallacy, as Sir THOMAS BROWNE[3] says, is "not the daughter of latter times, but an old and grey-headed errour, even in the days of ARISTOTLE," who deals with the story as he received it from CTESIAS, by whom it

[1] Machlis (said to be derived from *α*, priv., and *κλίνω*, *cubo*, quod non cubat). "Moreover in the island of Scandinavia there is a beast called *Machlis*, that hath neither ioynt in the hough, nor posternes in his hind legs, and therefore he never lieth down, but sleepeth leaning to a tree, wherefore the hunters that lie in wait for these beasts cut downe the trees while they are asleepe, and so take them; otherwise they should never be taken, they are so swift of foot that it is wonderful." (PLINY, *Natur. Hist.* Transl. Philemon Holland, book viii. ch. xv. p. 200.)

[2] "Sunt item quæ appellantur *Alces.* Harum est consimilis capreis figura, et varietas pellium; sed magnitudine paulo antecedunt, mutilæque sunt cornibus, *et crura sine nodis articulisque habent;* neque quietis causa procumbunt; neque, si quo afflictæ casu considerunt, erigere sese aut sublevare possunt. His sunt arbores pro cubilibus; ad eas sese applicant, atque ita, paulum modo reclinatæ, quietem capiunt, quarum ex vestigiis cum est animadversum a venatoribus, quo se recipere consueverint, omnes eo loco, aut a radicibus subruunt aut accidunt arbores tantum, ut summa species earum stantium relinquatur. Huc cum se consuetudine reclinaverint, infirmas arbores pondere affligunt, atque una ipsæ concidunt." (CÆSAR, *De Bello Gall.* lib. vi. ch. xxvii.)

The same fiction was extended by the early Arabian travellers to the rhinoceros, and in the MS. of the voyages of the "*Two Mahometans*," it is stated that the rhinoceros of Sumatra "n'a point d'articulation au genou ni à la main." (*Relations des Voyages, etc.* Paris, 1845, vol. i. p. 29.)

[3] EVELYN, who was a contemporary and friend of Sir Thomas Browne, observes in his diary, August 13, 1641, on arriving at Rotterdam, "here I first saw an elephant: it was a beast of a monstrous size, yet as flexible and nimble in the joints, contrary to the vulgar tradition, as could be imagined from so prodigious a bulk and strange fabric." (Vol. i. p. 20.)

appears to have been embodied in his lost work on India. But although ARISTOTLE generally receives the credit of having exposed and demolished the fallacy of CTESIAS,[1] it will be seen by a reference to his treatise *On the Progressive Motions of Animals*, that in reality he approached the question with some hesitation, and has not only left it doubtful in one passage whether the elephant has joints in his knee, although he demonstrates that it has joints in the shoulders;[2] but in another he distinctly affirms that on account of his weight the elephant cannot bend his forelegs together, but only one at a time, and reclines to sleep on that particular side.[3]

So great was the authority of ARISTOTLE, that ÆLIAN, who wrote two centuries later and borrowed many of his statements from the works of his predecessor, perpetuates this error; and, after describing the exploits of the trained elephants exhibited at Rome, adds the expression of his surprise, that an animal without joints (*ἄναρ-*

[1] In his *Natural History*, ARISTOTLE speaks of Ctesias as οὐκ ὢν ἀξιόπιστος. (L. viii. c. 27.)

[2] "When an animal moves progressively an hypothenuse is produced, which is equal in power to the magnitude that is quiescent, and to that which is intermediate. But since the members are equal, it is necessary that the member which is quiescent should be inflected either in the knee or in the incurvation, *if the animal that walks is without knees.* It is possible, however, for the leg to be moved, when not inflected, in the same manner as infants creep; and there is an ancient report of this kind about elephants, which is not true, for such animals as these, *are moved in consequence of an inflection taking place either in their shoulders or hips.*" (ARISTOTLE, *De Ingressu Anim.* ch. ix. Taylor's Transl.)

[3] ARISTOTLE, *De Animal.* lib. ii. ch. i. It is curious that Taylor, in his translation of this passage, was so strongly imbued with the "grey-headed errour," that in order to elucidate the somewhat obscure meaning of Aristotle, he has actually interpolated the text with the exploded fallacy of Ctesias, and after the word reclining to sleep, has inserted the words "*leaning against some wall or tree,*" which are not to be found in the original.

θρον) should yet be able to dance.[1] The fiction was too agreeable to be readily abandoned by the poets of the Lower Empire and the Romancers of the middle ages; and PHILE, a contemporary of PETRARCH and DANTE, who in the early part of the fourteenth century addressed his didactic poem on the elephant to the emperor Andronicus II., untaught by the exposition of ARISTOTLE, still clung to the old delusion,

Πόδες δὲ τούτῳ θαῦμα καὶ σαφὲς τέρας,
Οὓς, οὐ καθάπερ τἄλλα τῶν ζώων γένη,
Εἴωθε κινεῖν ἐξ ἀνάρθρων κλασμάτων·
Καὶ γὰρ στιβαροῖς συντεθέντες ὀστέοις,
Καὶ τῇ πλαδαρᾷ τῶν σφυρῶν καταστάσει,
Καὶ τῇ πρὸς ἄρθρα τῶν σκελῶν ὑποκρίσει,
Νῦν εἰς τόνους ἄγουσι, νῦν εἰς ὑφέσεις,
Τὰς παντοδαπὰς ἐκδρομὰς τοῦ θηρίου.
* * * * *
Βραχυτέρους ὄντας δὲ τῶν ὀπισθίων
'Αναμφιλέκτως οἶδα τοὺς ἐμπροσθίους·
Τούτοις ἐλέφας ἐνταθεὶς ὥσπερ στύλοις
'Ορθοστάδην ἄκαμπτος ὑπνώττων μένει.

v. 106, &c.

SOLINUS introduced the same fable into his *Polyhistor*; and DICUIL, the Irish commentator of the ninth century, who had an opportunity of seeing the elephant sent by Haroun Alraschid as a present to Charlemagne[2] in the year 802, corrects the error, and attributes its perpetuation to the circumstance that the joints in the elephant's leg are not very apparent, except when he lies down.[3]

[1] Ζῷον δὲ ἄναρθρον συνιέναι καὶ ῥυθμοῦ καὶ μέλους, καὶ φυλάττειν σχῆμα φύσεως δῶρα ταῦτα ἅμα καὶ ἰδιότης καθ' ἕκαστον ἐκπληκτική. (ÆLIAN, *De Nat. Anim.* lib. ii. cap. xi.)

[2] EGINHARD, *Vita Karoli*, c. xvi. and *Annales Francorum*, A.D. 810.

[3] "Sed idem Jullus, unum de elephantibus mentiens, falso loquitur; dicens elephantem nunquam jacere; dum ille sicut bos certissime jacet, ut populi communiter regni Francorum elephantem, in tempore Imperatoris Karoli, viderunt. Sed, forsitan, ideo hoc de elephante ficte æstimando scriptum est, eo quod genua et suffragines sui nisi quando jacet, non palam apparent." (DICUILUS, *De Mensura Orbis Terræ*, c. vii.)

It is a strong illustration of the vitality of error, that the delusion thus exposed by Dicuil in the ninth century, was revived by MATTHEW PARIS in the thirteenth ; and stranger still, that Matthew not only saw but made a drawing of the elephant presented to King Henry III. by the King of France in 1255, in which he nevertheless represents the legs as without joints.[1]

In the numerous mediæval treatises on natural history, known under the title of *Bestiaries*, this delusion regarding the elephant is often repeated ; and it is given at length in a metrical version of the *Physiologus* of THEORALDUS, amongst the Arundel Manuscripts in the British Museum.[2]

[1] *Cotton MSS.* NERO. D. I. fol. 168, b.

[2] *Arundel MSS.* No. 292, fol. 4, &c. It has been printed in the *Reliquiæ Antiquæ*, vol. i. p. 208, by Mr. WRIGHT, to whom I am indebted for the following rendering of the passage referred to:—

in water ge sal stonden
in water to mid side
ðat wanne hire harde tide
ðat ge ne falle niðer nogt
ðat it most in hire ðogt
for he ne haven no lið
ðat he mugen risen wið, etc.

"They will stand in the water,
in water up to the middle of the side,
that when it comes to them hard,
they may not fall down:
that is most in their thought,
for they have no joint
to enable them to rise again.
How he resteth him this animal,
when he walketh abroad,
hearken how it is here told.
For he is all unwieldy,
forsooth he seeks out a tree,
that is strong and steadfast,
and leans confidently against it,
when he is weary of walking.
The hunter has observed this,
who seeks to ensnare him,
where his usual dwelling is,
to do his will;
saws this tree and props it
in the manner that he best may,
covers it well that he (the elephant)
may not be on his guard.
Then he makes thereby a seat,
himself sits alone and watches
whether his trap takes effect.
Then cometh this unwieldy elephant,
and leans him on his side,
rests against the tree in the shadow,
and so both fall together.
if nobody be by when he falls,
he roars ruefully and calls for help,
roars ruefully in his manner,
hopes he shall through help rise.
Then cometh there one (elephant) in haste,
hopes he shall cause him to stand up;
labours and tries all his might,
but he cannot succeed a bit.
He knows then no other remedy,

With the Provençal song writers, the helplessness of the fallen elephant was a favourite simile, and amongst others RICHARD DE BARBEZIEUX, in the latter half of the twelfth century, sung,[1]

> "Atressi cum l'olifans
> Que quan chai no s' pot levar."

As elephants were but rarely seen in Europe prior to the seventeenth century, there were but few opportunities of correcting the popular fallacy by ocular demonstration. Hence SHAKSPEARE still believed that,

> "The elephant hath joints; but none for courtesy;
> His legs are for necessity, not flexure:"[2]

and DONNE sang of

> "Nature's great masterpiece, an elephant;
> The only harmless great thing:

---

but roars with his brother,
many and large (elephants) come there in search,
thinking to make him get up,
but for the help of them all
he may not get up.
Then they all roar one roar,
like the blast of a horn or the sound of bell;
for their great roaring
a young one cometh running,
stoops immediately to him,
puts his snout under him,
and asks the help of them all;
this elephant they raise on his legs:
and thus fails this hunter's trick,
in the manner that I have told you."

[1] One of the most venerable authorities by whom the fallacy was transmitted to modern times was PHILIP DE THAUN, who wrote, about the year 1121, A.D. his *Livre des Créatures*, dedicated to Adelaide of Louvaine, Queen of Henry I. of England. In the copy of it printed by the Historical Society of Science in 1841, and edited by Mr. WRIGHT, the following passage occurs:—

"Et Ysidres nus dit ki le elefant descrit,
* * * *
Es jambes par nature nen ad que une jointure,
Il ne pot pas gesir quant il se volt dormir,
Ke si cuchet estait par sei nen leverait;
Pur çeo li stot apuier, el lui del cucher,
U à arbre u à mur, idunc dort aseur.
E le gent de la terre, ki li volent conquere,
Li mur enfunderunt, u le arbre enciserunt;
Quant li elefant vendrat, ki s'i apuierat,
La arbre u le mur carrat, e il tribucherat;
Issi faiterement le parnent cele gent."

P. 100.

[2] *Troilus and Cressida*, act II. sc. 3. A.D. 1609.

> Yet Nature hath given him no knee to bend:
> Himself he up-props, on himself relies;
> Still sleeping stands."[1]

Sir THOMAS BROWNE, while he argues against the delusion, does not fail to record his suspicion, that "although the opinion at present be reasonably well suppressed, yet from the strings of tradition and fruitful recurrence of errour, it was not improbable it might revive in the next generation;"[2]—an anticipation which has proved singularly correct; for the heralds still continued to explain that the elephant is the emblem of watchfulness, "*nec jacet in somno*,"[3] and poets almost of our own times paint the scene when

> "Peaceful, beneath primeval trees, that cast
> Their ample shade on Niger's yellow stream,
> Or where the Ganges rolls his sacred waves,
> *Leans* the huge elephant."[4]

It is not difficult to discern whence this antiquated delusion took its origin; nor is it, as Sir THOMAS BROWNE imagined, to be traced exclusively "to the grosse and cylindricall structure" of the animal's legs. The fact is, that the elephant, returning in the early morning from his nocturnal revels in the reservoirs and watercourses, is accustomed to rub his muddy sides against a tree, and sometimes against a rock if more convenient. Often in my rides at sunrise through the northern forests, the

[1] *Progress of the Soul*, A.D. 1633.

[2] Sir T. BROWNE, *Vulgar Errors*, A.D. 1646.

[3] RANDAL HOME'S *Academy of Armory*, A.D. 1671. HOME only perpetuated the error of GUILLIM, who wrote his *Display of Heraldry* in A.D. 1610; wherein he explains that the elephant is "so proud of his strength that he never bows himself to any (*neither indeed can he*), and when he is once down he cannot rise up again." (Sec. III. ch. xii. p. 147.)

[4] THOMSON'S *Seasons*, A.D. 1728.

natives of Ceylon have pointed out that the elephants which had preceded me must have been of considerable size, judging from the height at which their marks had been left on the trees against which they had recently been rubbing. Not unfrequently the animals themselves, overcome with drowsiness from the night's gambolling, are found dozing and resting against the trees they had so visited, and in the same manner they have been discovered by sportsmen asleep, and leaning against a rock.

It is scarcely necessary to explain that the position is accidental, and that it is taken by the elephant not from any difficulty in lying at length on the ground, but rather from the coincidence that the structure of his legs affords such support in a standing position, that reclining scarcely adds to his enjoyment of repose; and elephants in a state of captivity have been known for months together to sleep without lying down.[1] So distinctive is this formation, and so self-sustaining the configuration of the limbs, that an elephant shot in the brain, by Major Rogers in 1836, was killed so instantaneously that it died literally *on its knees*, and remained resting on them. About the year 1826, Captain Dawson, the engineer of the great road to Kandy, over the Kaduganava pass, shot an elephant at Hangwelle on the banks of the

[1] So little is the elephant inclined to lie down in captivity, and even after hard labour, that the keepers are generally disposed to suspect illness when he betakes himself to this posture. PHILE, in his poem *De Animalium Proprietate*, attributes the propensity of the elephant to sleep on his legs, to the difficulty he experiences in rising to his feet:

'Ορθοστάδην δὲ καὶ καθεύδει παννύχως
Ὅτ' οὐκ ἀναστῆσαι μὲν εὐχερῶς πέλει.

But this is a misapprehension.

Kalany Ganga ; *it remained on its feet*, but so motionless, that after discharging a few more balls, he was induced to go close to it, and found it dead.

The real peculiarity in the elephant in lying down is, that he extends his hind legs backwards as a man does when he kneels, instead of bringing them under him like the horse or any other quadruped. The wise purpose of this arrangement must be obvious to any one who observes the struggle with which the horse *gets up* from the ground, and the violent efforts which he makes to raise himself erect. Such an exertion in the case of the elephant, and the force requisite to apply a similar movement to raise his weight (equal to four or five tons) would be attended with a dangerous strain upon the muscles, and hence the simple arrangement, which by enabling him to draw the hind feet gradually under him, assists him to rise without a perceptible effort.

From the same causes I am disposed to think that the elephant is too weighty and unwieldy to leap, at least to any considerable height or distance ; and yet I have seen in the *Colombo Observer* for March, 1866, an interesting account of a corral, written by an able and accurate describer, in which it is stated that an enfuriated tusker, the property of the Government, made a rush to escape from the enclosure, "and fairly leaped the barrier, of some fifteen feet high, only carrying away the top cross beam with a great crash."

The same construction renders his gait not a "gallop," as it has been somewhat loosely described,[1] which would

[1] *Menageries, etc.* "The Elephant," ch. i. Sir CHARLES BELL, in his essay on *The Hand and its Mechanism*, which

be too violent a motion for so vast a body; but a shuffle, that he can increase at pleasure to a pace as rapid as that of a man at full speed, but which he cannot maintain for any considerable distance.

It is to the structure of the knee-joint that the elephant is indebted for his singular facility in ascending and descending steep acclivities, climbing rocks and traversing precipitous ledges, where even a mule dare not venture; and this again leads to the correction of another generally received error, that his legs are "formed more for

forms one of the "Bridgewater Treatises," has exhibited the reasons deducible from organisation, which show the incapacity of the elephant to *spring* or *leap* like the horse and other animals whose structure is designed to facilitate agility and speed. In them the various bones of the shoulder and fore limbs, especially the clavicle and humerus, are set at such an angle, that the shock in descending is modified, and the joints and sockets protected from the injury

occasioned by concussion. But in the elephant, where the weight of the body is immense, the bones of the leg, in order to present solidity and strength to sustain it, are built in one firm and perpendicular column; instead of being placed somewhat obliquely at their points of contact. Thus whilst the force of the weight in descending is broken and distributed by this arrangement in the case of the horse; it would be so concentrated in the elephant as to endanger every joint from the toe to the shoulder.

strength than flexibility, and fitted to bear an enormous weight upon a level surface, without the necessity of ascending or descending great acclivities."[1] The same authority assumes that, although the elephant is found in the neighbourhood of mountainous ranges, and will even ascend rocky passes, such a service is a violation of its natural habits.

Of the elephant of Africa I am not qualified to speak, nor of the nature of the ground which it most frequents; but certainly the facts in connection with the elephant of India are all irreconcilable with the theory mentioned above. In Bengal, in the Nilgherries, in Nepal, in Burmah, in Siam, Sumatra, and Ceylon, the districts in which the elephants most abound, are all hilly and mountainous. In the latter, especially, there is not a range so elevated as to be inaccessible to them. On the very summit of Adam's Peak, at an altitude of 7,420 feet, and on a pinnacle which the pilgrims climb with difficulty, by means of steps hewn in the rock, Major Skinner, in 1840, found the spoor of an elephant.

Prior to 1840, and before coffee-plantations had been extensively opened in the Kandyan ranges, there was not a mountain or a lofty feature of land of Ceylon which they had not traversed, in their periodical migrations in search of water; and the sagacity which they display in "laying out roads" is almost incredible. They generally keep along the *backbone* of a chain of hills, avoiding steep gradients: and one curious observation was not lost upon the Government surveyors, that in crossing

[1] *Menageries, etc.* "The Elephant," ch. ii.

valleys from ridge to ridge, through forests so dense as to obstruct a distant view, the elephants invariably select the line of march which communicates most judiciously with the opposite point, by means of the safest ford.[1] So sure-footed are they, that there are few places where man can go that an elephant cannot follow, provided there be space to admit his bulk, and solidity to sustain his weight.

In 1865 a capture of elephants was attempted at Avisavelle in Ceylon: the corral was constructed close to a wall of rocks so precipitous and high that it was considered superfluous to continue the enclosure in front of them. But over these rocks the elephants made their escape, and the corral was a total failure.[2]

This faculty is almost entirely derived from the unusual position, as compared with other quadrupeds, of the knee joint of the hind leg; arising from the superior length of the thigh bone, and the shortness of the metatarsus: the heel being almost where it projects in man, instead of being lifted up as a "hock." It is this which enables him, in descending declivities, to depress and adjust the weight of his hinder portions, which would otherwise overbalance and force him headlong.[3] It is

[1] Dr. HOOKER, in describing the ascent of the Himalayas, says, the natives in making their paths despise all zigzags, and run in straight lines up the steepest hill faces; whilst "the elephant's path is an excellent specimen of engineering—the opposite of the native track,—for it winds judiciously." (*Himalayan Journal*, vol. i. ch. iv.)

[2] *Ceylon Observer*, March 1865.

[3] Since the above passage was written, I have seen in the *Journal of the Asiatic Society of Bengal*, vol. xiii. pt. ii. p. 916, a paper upon this subject, illustrated by the subjoined diagram.

The writer says, "an elephant descending a bank of too acute an angle to admit of his walking down it direct, (which, were he to attempt, his huge

by the same arrangement that he is enabled, on uneven ground, to lift his feet, which are tender and sensitive, with delicacy, and plant them with such decision as to

body, soon disarranging the centre of gravity, would certainly topple over,) proceeds thus. His first manœuvre is to kneel down close to the edge of the declivity, placing his chest to the ground: one fore leg is then cautiously passed a short way down the slope; and if there is no natural protection to afford a firm footing, he speedily forms one by stamping into the soil if moist, or kicking out a footing if dry. This point gained, the other fore leg is brought down in the same way; and performs the same work, a little in advance of the first; which is thus at liberty to move lower still. Then,, first

one and then the second of the hind legs is carefully drawn over the side, and the hind feet in turn occupy the resting-places previously used and left by the fore ones. The course, however, in such precipitous ground is not straight from top to bottom, but slopes along the face of the bank, descending till the animal gains the level below. This an elephant has done, at an angle of 45 degrees, carrying a *howdah*, its occupant, his attendant, and sporting apparatus; and in a much less time than it takes to describe the operation." I have observed that an elephant in descending a declivity uses his knees, on the side next the bank; and his feet on the lower side only.

ensure his own safety as well as that of objects which it is expedient to avoid touching.

A *herd* of elephants is a family, not a group whom accident or attachment may have induced to associate together. Similarity of features and caste attest that, among the various individuals which compose it, there is a common lineage and relationship. In a herd of twenty-one elephants, captured in 1844, the trunks of each individual presented the same peculiar formation, —long, and almost of one uniform breadth throughout, instead of tapering gradually from the root to the nostril. In another instance, the eyes of thirty-five taken in one corral were of the same colour in each. The same slope of the back, the same form of the forehead, is to be detected in the majority of the same group.

In the forest several herds sometimes browse in close contiguity, and in their expeditions in search of water they may form a body of possibly one or two hundred; but on the slightest disturbance each distinct herd hastens to re-form within its own particular circle, and to take measures on its own behalf for retreat or defence.

The natives of any place which may chance to be frequented by elephants, observe that the numbers of the same herd fluctuate very slightly; and hunters in pursuit of them, who may chance to have shot one or more, always reckon with certainty the precise number of those remaining, although a considerable interval may intervene before they again encounter them. The proportion of males is generally small, and some herds have been seen composed exclusively of females; possibly in consequence of the males having been shot. A herd usually consists of from ten to twenty individuals, though occasionally they exceed the latter number; and in their frequent migrations and nightly resort to tanks and water-courses, alliances are formed between members of associated herds, which serve to introduce new blood into the family.

In illustration of the attachment of the elephant to its young, the authority of KNOX has been quoted, that "the shees are alike tender of anyone's young ones as of their own."[1] Their affection in this particular is undoubted, but I question whether it exceeds that of other animals; and the trait thus adduced of their indiscriminate kindness to all the young of the herd, —of which I have myself been an eye-witness,—so far from being an evidence of the intensity of parental attachment individually, is, perhaps, somewhat inconsistent with the existence of such a passion to any extraordinary degree.[2] In fact, some individuals, who

[1] A correspondent of Buffon, M. MARCELLUS BLES, Seigneur de Moergestal, who resided eleven years in Ceylon in the time of the Dutch, says in one of his communications, that in herds of forty or fifty, enclosed in a single corral, there were frequently very young calves; and that "on ne pouvoit pas reconnoître quelles étoient les mères de chacun de ces petits éléphans, car tous ces jeunes animaux paroissent faire manse commune; ils têtent indistinctement celles des femelles de toute la troupe qui ont du lait, soit qu'elles aient elles-mêmes un petit en propre, soit qu'elles n'en aient point." (BUFFON, *Suppl. à l'Hist. des Anim.* vol. vi. p. 25.)

[2] WHITE, in his *Natural History of Selbourne*, philosophising on the fact which had fallen under his own notice of this indiscriminate suckling of the young of one animal by the parent of another, is disposed to ascribe it to a selfish feeling; the pleasure and relief of having its distended teats drawn by this intervention. He notices the circumstance of a leveret having been thus nursed by a cat, whose kittens had been recently drowned; and observes that "this strange affection was probably occasioned by that desiderium,

have had extensive facilities for observation, doubt whether the fondness of the female elephants for their offspring is so great as that of many other animals; as instances are not wanting in Ceylon, in which, when pursued by the hunters, the herd has abandoned the young ones in their flight, notwithstanding the cries of the latter for protection.

In an interesting paper on the habits of the Indian elephant, published in the *Philosophical Transactions for* 1793, Mr. CORSE says: "If a wild elephant happens to be separated from its young for only two days, though giving suck, she never after recognises or acknowledges it," although the young one evidently knows its dam, and by its plaintive cries and submissive approaches solicits her assistance.

If by any accident an elephant becomes hopelessly separated from his own herd, he is not permitted to attach himself to any other. He may browse in their vicinity, or resort to the same places to drink and to bathe; but the intercourse is only on a distant and conventional footing, and no familiarity or intimate association is under any circumstances permitted. To such

those tender maternal feelings, which the loss of her kittens had awakened in her breast; and by the complacency and ease she derived to herself from procuring her teats to be drawn, which were too much distended with milk; till from habit she became as much delighted with this foundling as if it had been her real offspring. This incident is no bad solution of that strange circumstance which grave historians, as well as the poets, assert of exposed children being sometimes nurtured by female wild beasts that probably had lost their young. For it is not one whit more marvellous that Romulus and Remus in their infant state should be nursed by a she wolf than that a poor little suckling leveret should be fostered and cherished by a bloody Grimalkin." (WHITE's *Selborne*, lett. xx.) General SLEAMAN in his narrative of a journey through Oude gives some remarkable narratives of children suckled by wolves and found associating with their cubs.

a height is this exclusiveness carried, that even amidst the terror and stupefaction of an elephant corral, when an individual, detached from his own party in the *mêlée* and confusion, has been driven into the enclosure along with an unbroken herd, I have seen him repulsed in every attempt to take refuge among them, and driven off by heavy blows with their trunks as often as he attempted to insinuate himself within the circle which they had formed for their own security. There can be no reasonable doubt that this jealous and exclusive policy not only contributes to produce, but mainly serves to perpetuate, the class of solitary elephants which are known by the term *goondahs*, in India, and which from their vicious propensities and predatory habits are called *Hora*, or *Rogues*, in Ceylon.[1]

It is believed by the Singhalese that these are either individuals, who by accident have lost their former associates and become morose and savage from rage and solitude; or else that being naturally vicious they have become daring from the yielding habits of their milder companions, and eventually separated themselves from the rest of the herd which had refused to associate with

[1] The term "rogue" is scarcely sufficiently accounted for by supposing it to be the English equivalent for the Singhalese word *Hora*. In that very curious book, the *Life and Adventures of* JOHN CHRISTOPHER WOLF, *late principal Secretary at Jaffnapatam in Ceylon*, see *ante*, note, p. 31, the author says, when a male elephant in a quarrel about the females "is beat out of the field and obliged to go without a consort, he becomes furious and mad, killing every living creature, be it man or beast; and in this state is called *ronkedor*, an object of greater terror to a traveller than a hundred wild ones." (P. 142.) In another passage, p. 164, he is called *runkedor*, and I have seen it spelt elsewhere *ronquedue*. WOLF does not give "*ronkedor*" as a term peculiar to that section of the island; but both there and elsewhere, it is obsolete at the present day, unless it be open to conjecture that the modern term "rogue" is a modification of *ronquedue*.

them. Another conjecture is, that being almost universally males, the death or capture of particular females may have detached them from their former companions in search of fresh alliances.[1] It is also believed that a tame elephant escaping from activity, unable to rejoin its former herd, and excluded from any other, becomes a "*rogue*" from necessity. In Ceylon it is generally believed that the *rogues* are all males (but of this I am not certain), and so sullen is their disposition that although two may be in the same vicinity, there is no known instance of two *rogues* associating, or of a *rogue* being seen in company with another elephant.

They spend their nights in marauding, often around the dwellings of men, destroying plantations, trampling down gardens, and committing serious ravages in rice grounds and young coco-nut plantations. Hence from their closer contact with man and his dwellings, these outcasts become disabused of many of the terrors which render the ordinary elephant timid and needlessly cautious; they break through fences without fear; and even in the daylight a *rogue* has been known near Ambogammoa to watch a field of labourers at work in reaping rice, and boldly to walk in amongst them, seize a sheaf from the heap, and retire with it leisurely to the jungle. By day they generally seek concealment, but are fre-

[1] BUCHANAN, in his *Survey of Bhagulpore*, p. 503, says that solitary males of the wild buffalo, "when driven from the herd by stronger competitors for female society, are reckoned very dangerous to meet with; for they are apt to wreak their vengeance on whatever they meet, and are said to kill annually three or four people." LIVINGSTONE relates the same of the solitary hippopotamus, which becomes soured in temper, and wantonly attacks the passing canoes. (*Travels in South Africa*, p. 231.)

quently to be met with prowling about the by-roads and jungle paths, where travellers are exposed to the utmost risk from their assaults. It is probable that this hostility to man is the result of the enmity engendered by measures which the natives, who have a constant dread of their visits, adopt for the protection of the growing crops. In some districts, especially in the low country of Badulla, the villagers occasionally enclose their cottages with rude walls of earth and branches to protect them from nightly assaults. In places infested by them, the visits of European sportsmen to the vicinity of their haunts are eagerly encouraged by the natives, who think themselves happy in lending their services to track the herds in consideration of the benefit conferred on the village communities by the destruction of a rogue. In 1847 one of these formidable creatures frequented for some months the Rangbodde Pass on the great mountain road leading to the sanatarium, at Neuera-ellia; and amongst other excesses, killed a Caffre belonging to the corps of Caffre pioneers, by seizing him with its trunk and beating him to death against the bank.

To return to the herd: one member of it, usually the largest and most powerful, is by common consent implicitly followed as leader. A tusker, if there be one in the party, is generally observed to be the commander; but a female, if of superior energy, is as readily obeyed as a male. In fact, in this promotion there is no reason to doubt that supremacy is almost unconsciously assumed by those endowed with superior vigour and courage rather than from the accidental possession of greater bodily strength; and the devotion and loyalty which the herd evince to their leader are very remarkable. This is more readily seen in the case of a tusker than any other, because in a herd he is generally the object of the keenest pursuit by the hunters. On such occasions the others do their utmost to protect him from danger: when driven to extremity they place their leader in the centre and crowd so eagerly in front of him that the sportsmen have to shoot a number which they might otherwise have spared. In one instance a tusker, which was badly wounded by Major ROGERS, was promptly surrounded by his companions, who supported him between their shoulders, and actually succeeded in covering his retreat to the forest.

Those who have lived much in the jungle in Ceylon, and had constant opportunities of watching the habits of wild elephants, have witnessed instances of the submission of herds to their leaders, that suggest an inquiry of singular interest as to the means adopted by the latter to communicate with distinctness, orders which are observed with the most implicit obedience by their followers. The following narrative of an adventure in the great central forest toward the north of the island, communicated to me by Major SKINNER, who was engaged for some time in surveying and opening roads through the thickly-wooded districts there, will serve better than any abstract description to convey an idea of the conduct of a herd on such occasions:—

"The case you refer to struck me as exhibiting something more than ordinary brute instinct, and approached nearer to reasoning powers than any other instance I can now remember. I cannot do justice to the scene, although it appeared to me at the time to be so remarkable that it left a deep impression in my mind.

"In the height of the dry season in Neuera-Kalawa, you know the streams are all dried up, and the tanks nearly so. All animals are then sorely pressed for water, and they congregate in the vicinity of those tanks in which there may remain ever so little of the precious element.

"During one of those seasons I was encamped on the bund or embankment of a very small tank, the water in which was so dried that its surface could not have exceeded an area of 500 square yards. It was the only pond within many miles, and I knew that of necessity a very large herd of elephants, which had been in the neighbourhood all day, must resort to it at night.

"On the lower side of the tank, and in a line with the embankment, was a thick forest, in which the elephants sheltered themselves during the day. On the upper side and all around the tank there was a considerable margin of open ground. It was one of those beautiful bright, clear, moonlight nights, when objects could be seen almost as distinctly as by day, and I determined to avail myself of the opportunity to observe the movements of the herd, which had already manifested some uneasiness at our presence. The locality was very favourable for my purpose, and an enormous tree projecting over the tank afforded me a secure lodgement in its branches. Having ordered the fires of my camp to be extinguished at an early hour, and all my followers to retire to rest, I took up my post of observation on the overhanging bough; but I had to remain for upwards of two hours before anything was to be seen or heard of the elephants, although I knew they were within 500 yards of me. At length, about the distance of 300 yards from the water, an unusually large elephant issued from the dense cover, and advanced cautiously across the open ground to within 100 yards of the tank, where he stood perfectly motionless. So quiet had the elephants become (although they had been roaring and breaking the jungle throughout the day and evening), that not a movement was now to be heard. The huge vidette remained in his position, still as a rock, for a few minutes, and then made three successive stealthy advances of several yards (halting for some minutes between each, with ears bent forward to catch the slightest sound), and in this way he moved slowly up to the water's edge. Still he did not venture to quench his thirst, for though his fore feet were partially in the tank and his vast body was reflected clear in the water, he remained for some minutes listening in perfect stillness. Not a motion could be perceived in himself or his shadow. He returned cautiously and slowly to the position he had at first taken up on emerging from the forest. Here in a little while he was joined by five others, with which he again proceeded as cautiously, but less slowly than before, to within a few yards of the tank, and then posted his patrols. He then re-entered the forest and collected around him the whole herd, which must have amounted to between 80 and 100 individuals,—led them across the open ground with the most extraordinary composure and quietness, till he joined the advanced guard, when he left them for a moment and repeated his former reconnoissance at the edge of the tank. After which, having apparently satisfied himself that all was safe, he returned and obviously gave the order to advance, for in a moment the whole herd rushed into the water with a degree of unreserved confidence, so opposite to the caution and timidity which had marked their previous movements, that nothing will ever persuade me that there was not rational and preconcerted co-operation throughout the whole party, and a degree of responsible authority exercised by the patriarch leader.

"When the poor animals had gained possession of the tank (the leader being the last to enter), they seemed to abandon themselves to enjoyment without restraint or apprehension of danger. Such a mass of animal life I had never before seen huddled together in so narrow a space. It seemed to me as though they would have nearly drunk the tank dry. I watched them with great interest until they had satisfied themselves as well in bathing as in drinking, when I tried how small a noise would apprise them of the proximity of unwelcome neighbours. I had but to break a little twig, and the solid mass instantly took to flight like a herd of frightened deer, each of the smaller calves being apparently shouldered and carried along between two of the older ones."[1]

[1] Letter from Major SKINNER.

In drinking, the elephant, like the camel, although preferring water pure, shows no decided aversion to it when discoloured with mud;[1] and the eagerness with which he precipitates himself into the tanks and streams attests his exquisite enjoyment of the fresh coolness, which to him is the chief attraction. In crossing deep rivers, although his rotundity and buoyancy enable him to swim with a less immersion than other quadrupeds, he generally prefers to sink till no part of his huge body is visible except the tip of his trunk, through which he breathes, moving beneath the surface, and only now and then raising his head to look that he is keeping the proper direction.[2] In the dry season the scanty streams which, during the rains, are sufficient to convert the rivers of the low country into torrents, often entirely disappear, leaving only broad expanses of dry sand,

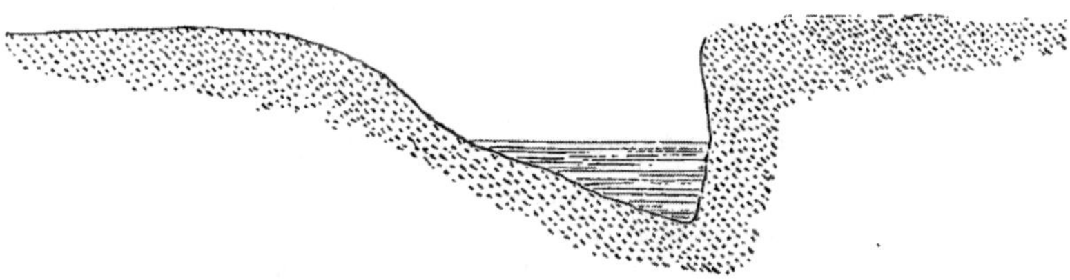

which they have swept down with them from the hills. In this the elephants contrive to sink wells for their

[1] This peculiarity was known in the middle ages, and PHILE, writing in the fourteenth century, says, that such is his *preference* for muddy water that the elephant *stirs it* before he drinks.

Ὕδωρ δὲ πίνει συγχυθὲν πρὶν ἂν πίνοι,
Τὸ γὰρ διειδὲς ἀκριβῶς διαπτύει.

PHILE *de Eleph.* l. 144.

[2] A tame elephant, when taken by his keepers to be bathed, and to have his skin washed and rubbed, lies down on his side, pressing his head to the bottom under water, with only the top of his trunk protruded, to breathe.

own use by scooping out the sand to the depth of four or five feet, and leaving a hollow for the percolation of the spring. But as the weight of the elephant would force in the side if left perpendicular, one approach is always formed with such a gradient that he can reach the water with his trunk without disturbing the surrounding sand.

I have reason to believe, although the fact has not been authoritatively stated by naturalists, that the stomach of the elephant will be found to include a chamber analogous to that possessed by some of the ruminants, calculated to contain a supply of water as a provision against emergencies. The fact of his being enabled to retain a quantity of water and discharge it at pleasure has been long known to every observer of the habits of the animal; but the proboscis has always been supposed to be "his water-reservoir,"[1] and the theory of an internal receptacle has not been discussed. The truth is that the anatomy of the elephant is even yet but imperfectly understood,[2] and, although some peculiarities of his

[1] BRODERIP'S *Zoological Recreations*, p. 259.

[2] For observing the osteology of the elephant, materials are of course abundant in the indestructible remains of the animal: but the study of the intestines, and the dissection of the softer parts by comparative anatomists in Europe, have been up to the present time beset by difficulties. These arise not alone from the rarity of subjects, but even in cases where elephants have died in these countries, decomposition interposes, and before the thorough examination of so vast a body can be satisfactorily completed, the great mass falls into putrefaction.

The principal English authorities are *An Anatomical Account of the Elephant accidentally burnt in Dublin*, by A. MOLYNEUX, A.D. 1696; which is probably a reprint of a letter on the same subject in the library of Trinity College, Dublin, addressed by A. Moulin to Sir William Petty, Lond. 1682. There are also some papers communicated to Sir Hans Sloane, and afterwards published in the *Philosophical Transactions* of the year 1710, by Dr. P. BLAIR, who had an opportunity of dissecting an

stomach were observed at an early period by ARISTOTLE and others ;[1] and even their configuration described, the function of the abnormal portion remained undetermined, and has been only recently conjectured. An elephant which belonged to Louis XIV. died at Versailles in 1681 at the age of seventeen, and an account of its dissection was published in the *Mémoires pour servir à l'Histoire Naturelle*, under the authority of the Academy of Sciences, in which the unusual appendages of the stomach are pointed out with sufficient particularity, but no suggestion is made as to their probable uses."[2]

elephant which died at Dundee in 1708. The latter writer observes that, "notwithstanding the vast interest attaching to the elephant in all ages, yet has its body been hitherto very little subjected to anatomical inquiries;" and he laments that the rapid decomposition of the carcase, and other causes, had interposed obstacles to the scrutiny of the subject he was so fortunate as to find access to.

In 1723 Dr. WM. STUCKLEY published *Some Anatomical Observations made upon the Dissection of an Elephant;* but each of the above essays is necessarily unsatisfactory, and little has since been done to supply their defects. One of the late and most valuable contributions to the subject, is a paper read before the Royal Irish Academy, on the 18th of Feb. 1847, by Professor HARRISON, who had the opportunity of dissecting an Indian elephant which died of acute fever; but the examination, so far as he has made it public, extends only to the cranium, the brain, and the proboscis, the larynx, trachea, and œsophagus. An essential service would be rendered to science if some sportsman in Ceylon, or some of the officers connected with the elephant establishment there, would take the trouble to forward the carcase of a young one to England in a state fit for dissection.

Postscriptum.—I am happy to say that a young elephant, carefully preserved in spirits, has recently been obtained in Ceylon, and forwarded to Prof. Owen, of the British Museum, by the joint exertions of M. DIARD and Major SKINNER. An opportunity has thus been afforded of which science will reap the advantage, of devoting a patient attention to the internal structure of this most interesting animal.

[1] ARISTOTLE noticed a peculiarity in the intestinal configuration of the elephant such as gave it the appearance of having four stomachs. *De Anim. Hist.* l. ii. c. 17.

[2] The passage as quoted by BUFFON from the *Mémoires* is as follows:—"L'estomac avoit peu de diamètre; il en avoit moins que le colon, car son diamètre n'étoit que de quatorze pouces dans la partie la plus large; il avoit trois pieds et demi de longueur: l'orifice supérieur étoit à peu près aussi éloigné du pylore que du fond du grand cul-de-

A writer in the *Quarterly Review* for December 1850, says that "CAMPER and other comparative anatomists have shown that the left, or cardiac end of the stomach in the elephant is adapted, by several wide folds of lining membrane, to serve as a receiver for water;" but this is scarcely correct, for although CAMPER has accurately figured the external form of the stomach, he disposes of the question of the interior functions with the simple remark that its folds "semblent en faire une espèce de division particulière."[1] In like manner Sir EVERARD HOME, in his *Lectures on Comparative Anatomy*, has not only carefully described the form of the elephant's stomach, and furnished a drawing of it even more accurate than CAMPER; but he has equally failed to assign any purpose for so strange a formation; contenting himself with observing that the structure is a peculiarity, and that one of the remarkable folds nearest the orifice of the diaphragm appears to act as a valve, so that the portion beyond may be considered as an appendage similar to that of the hog and the *peccary*.[2]

sac qui se terminoit en une pointe composée de tuniques beaucoup plus épaisses que celles du reste de l'estomac; il y avoit au fond du grand cul-de-sac plusieurs feuillets épais d'une ligne, larges d'un pouce et demi, et disposés irrégulièrement; le reste des parois intérieures étoit percé de plusieurs petits trous et par de plus grands qui correspondoient à des grains glanduleux." (BUFFON, *Hist. Nat.* vol. xi. p. 109.)

[1] "L'extrémité voisine du cardiaque se termine par une poche très-considérable et doublée à l'intérieure de quatorze valvules orbiculaires qui semblent en faire une espèce de division particulière." (CAMPER, *Description anatomique d'un Eléphant mâle*, p. 37, tabl. IX.)

[2] "The elephant has another peculiarity in the internal structure of the stomach. It is longer and narrower than that of most animals. The cuticular membrane of the œsophagus terminates at the orifice of the stomach. At the cardiac end, which is very narrow and pointed at the extremity, the lining is thick and glandular, and is thrown into transverse folds, of which five are broad and nine narrow. That nearest the orifice of the œsophagus is the broadest, and appears to act occasionally as a valve, so that the part

The appendage thus alluded to by Sir EVERARD HOME is the "grand cul-de-sac," noticed by the Académie des Sciences, and the "division particulière," figured by CAMPER. It is of sufficient dimensions to contain ten gallons of water, and by means of the valve above alluded to, it can be shut off from the chamber devoted to the process of digestion. Professor OWEN is probably the first who, not from an autopsy, but from the mere

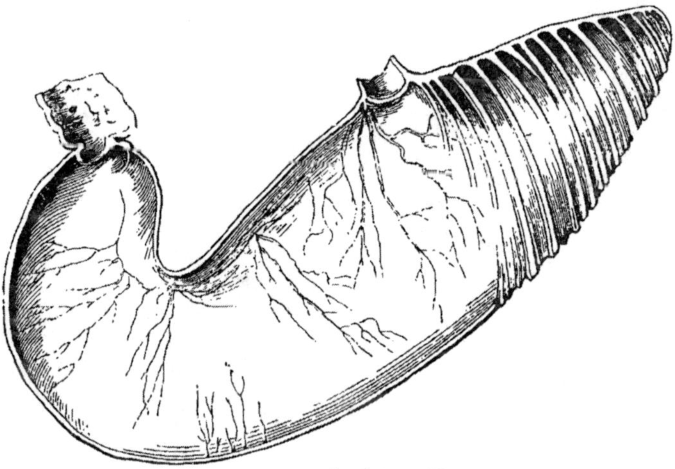

ELEPHANT'S STOMACH.

inspection of the drawings of CAMPER and HOME, ventured to assert (in lectures hitherto unpublished), that the uses of this section of the elephant's stomach may be analogous to those ascertained to belong to a somewhat similar arrangement in the stomach of the camel, one cavity of which is exclusively employed as a

beyond may be considered as an appendage similar to that of the peccary and the hog. The membrane of the cardiac portion is uniformly smooth; that of the pyloric is thicker and more vascular." (*Lectures on Comparative Anatomy*, by Sir EVERARD HOME, Bart. 4to. Lond. vol. i. p. 155. The figure of the elephant's stomach is given in his *Lectures*, vol. ii. plate xviii.)

reservoir for water, and performs no function in the preparation of food.[1]

Whilst Professor Owen was advancing this conjecture, another comparative anatomist, from the examination of another portion of the structure of the elephant, was led to a somewhat similar conclusion. Dr. Harrison of

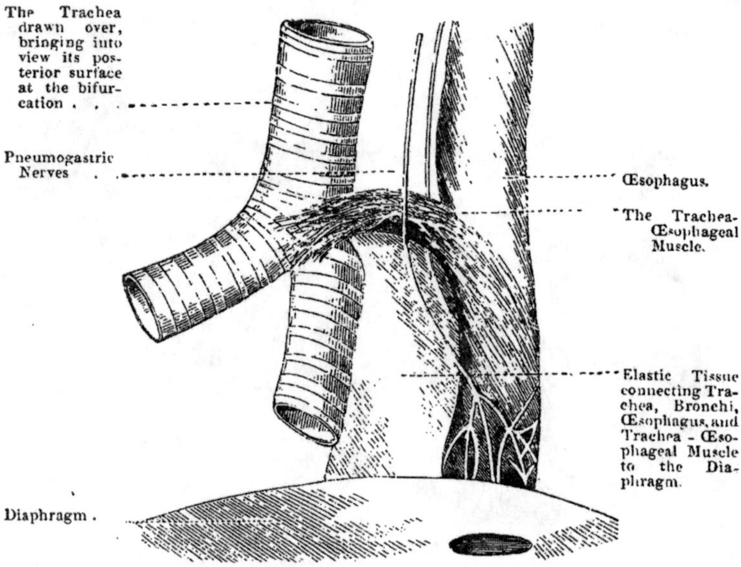

Dublin had, in 1847, an opportunity of dissecting the body of an elephant which had suddenly died; and in the course of his examination of the thoracic viscera he observed that an unusually close connection existed between the trachea and œsophagus, which he found to depend on a muscle unnoticed by any previous anatomist,

[1] A similar arrangement, with some modifications, has more recently been found in the llama of the Andes, which, like the camel, is used as a beast of burden in the Cordilleras of Chili and Peru: but both these and the camel are *ruminants*, whilst the elephant belongs to the Pachydermata.

connecting the back of the former with the fore part of the latter, along which the fibres descend and can be distinctly traced to the cardiac orifice of the stomach. Imperfectly acquainted with the habits and functions of the elephant in a state of nature, Dr. HARRISON found it difficult to pronounce as to the use of this very peculiar structure; but looking to the intimate connection between the mechanism concerned in the functions of respiration and deglutition, and seeing that the proboscis served in a double capacity as an instrument of voice and an organ for the prehension of food, he ventured (apparently without adverting to the abnormal form of the stomach) to express the opinion that this muscle, viewing its attachment to the trachea, might either have some influence in raising the diaphragm, and thereby assisting in expiration, "*or that it might raise the cardiac orifice of the stomach, and so aid this organ to regurgitate a portion of its contents into the œsophagus.*" [1]

Dr. HARRISON, on the reflection that "we have no satisfactory evidence that the animal ever ruminates," thought it useless to speculate on the latter supposition as to the action of the newly discovered muscle, and rather inclined to the surmise that it was designed to assist the elephant in producing the remarkable sound through his proboscis known as "trumpeting;" but there is little room to doubt that of the two the rejected hypothesis was the more correct one. I have elsewhere described the occurrence to which I was myself a witness, of elephants inserting their proboscis in their mouths,

[1] *Proceed. Roy. Irish. Acad.* vol. iv. p. 133.

and withdrawing gallons of water, which could only have been contained in the receptacle figured by CAMPER and HOME, and of which the true uses were discerned by the clear intellect of Professor OWEN. I was not, till very recently, aware that a similar observation as to this remarkable habit of the elephant, had been made by the author of the *Ayeen Akbery*, in his account of the *Feel Kaneh*, or elephant stables of the Emperor Akbar, in which he says, "an elephant frequently with his trunk takes water out of his stomach and sprinkles himself

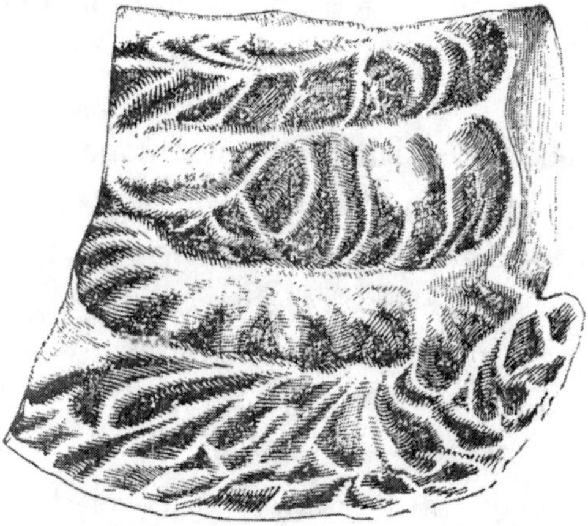

WATER-CELLS IN THE STOMACH OF THE CAMEL.

with it, and it is not in the least offensive.[1] FORBES, in his Oriental Memoirs, quotes this passage of the *Ayeen Akbery*, but without a remark ; nor does any European writer with whose works I am acquainted appear to have been cognisant of the peculiarity in question.

It is to be hoped that Professor OWEN'S dissection of

[1] *Ayeen Akbery*, transl. by GLADWIN, vol. i. pt. i. p. 147.

the young elephant, recently arrived, may serve to decide this highly interesting point.[1] Should scientific investigation hereafter more clearly establish the fact that, in this particular, the structure of the elephant is assimilated to that of the llama and the camel, it will be regarded as more than a mere coincidence, that an apparatus, so unique in its purpose and action, should have been conferred by the Creator on the three animals which in sultry climates are, by this arrangement, enabled to traverse arid regions in the service of man.[2] To show this peculiar organisation where it attains its fullest development, I have given a sketch of the water-cells in the stomach of the camel on the preceding page.

The *food* of the elephant is so abundant, that in eating he never appears to be impatient or voracious, but rather to play with the leaves and branches on which he leisurely feeds. In riding by places where a herd has recently halted, I have sometimes seen the bark peeled curiously off the twigs, as though it had been done in mere dalliance. In the same way in eating grass the elephant selects a tussac which he draws from the ground by a dexterous twist of his trunk, and nothing can be more graceful than the ease with which, before conveying

[1] One of the Indian names for the elephant is *duipa*, which signifies "to drink twice." (AMANDI, p. 513.) Can this have reference to the peculiarity of the stomach for retaining a supply of water? Or has it merely reference to the habit of the animal to fill his trunk before transferring the water to his mouth?

[2] The buffalo and the humped cattle of India, which are used for draught and burden, have, I believe, a development somewhat more conspicuous than in the rest of their congeners, of the organisation of the reticulum which enables the ruminants generally to endure thirst, and abstain from water, but nothing in them approaches in singularity of character to the distinct cavities in the stomach exhibited by the three animals above alluded to.

it to his mouth, he beats the earth from its roots by striking it gently upon his fore-leg. A coco-nut he first rolls under foot, to detach the strong outer bark, then stripping off with his trunk the thick layer of fibre within, he places the shell in his mouth, and swallows with evident relish the fresh liquid which flows as he crushes it between his grinders.

The natives of the peninsula of Jaffna always look for the periodical appearance of the elephants, at the precise time when the fruit of the palmyra palm begins to fall to the ground from ripeness. In like manner in the eastern provinces where the custom prevails of cultivating what is called *chena* [1] land (by clearing a patch of forest for the purpose of raising a single crop, after which the ground is abandoned, and reverts to jungle again), although a single elephant may not have been seen in the neighbourhood during the early stages of the process, the Moormen, who are the principal cultivators of this class, will predict their appearance with almost unerring confidence so soon as the grains shall have begun to ripen; and although the crop comes to maturity at different periods in different districts, herds are certain to be seen at each in succession, as soon as it is ready to be cut. In these well-timed excursions they resemble the bison of North America, which, by a similarly mysterious instinct, finds its way to portions of the distant prairies, where accidental fires have been followed by a growth of tender grass. In Ceylon, although the fences around these *chenas* are little more

[1] For an explanation of this term, see Sir J. EMERSON TENNENT'S *Ceylon, etc.* vol. i. p. 498.

than lines of reeds loosely fastened together, they are sufficient, with the presence of a single watcher, to prevent the entrance of the elephants, who wait patiently till the rice and *coracan* have been removed, and the watcher withdrawn; and, then finding gaps in the fence, they may be seen gleaning among the leavings and the stubble; and they take their departure when these are exhausted, apparently in the direction of some other *chena*, which they have ascertained to be about to be cut.

There is something still unexplained in the dread which an elephant always exhibits on approaching a fence, and the reluctance which he displays to face the slightest artificial obstruction to his passage. In the area of the fine old tank of Tissa-weva, close by Anarajapoora, the natives cultivate grain, during the dry season, around the margin where the ground has been left bare by the subsidence of the water. These little patches of rice they enclose with small sticks an inch in diameter and five or six feet in height, such as would scarcely serve to keep out a wild hog if he attempted to force his way through. Passages of from ten to twenty feet wide are left between each field, to permit the wild elephants, which abound in the vicinity, to make their nocturnal visits to the water still remaining in the centre of the tank. Night after night these open pathways are frequented by herds, but the tempting corn is never touched, nor is a single fence disturbed, although the merest movement of a trunk would be sufficient to demolish the fragile obstruction. Yet the same spots, the fences being left open as soon as the grain has been cut and carried home, are eagerly entered by the elephants to glean amongst the stubble.

Sportsmen observe that an elephant, even when enraged by a wound, will hesitate to charge an assailant across an intervening hedge, but will hurry along it to seek for an opening. It is possible that, on the part of the elephant, there may be some instinctive consciousness, that owing to his superior bulk, he is exposed to danger from sources that might be perfectly harmless in the case of lighter animals, and hence his suspicion that every fence may conceal a snare or pitfall. Some similar apprehension is apparent in the deer, which shrinks from attempting a fence of wire, although it will clear without hesitation a solid wall of greater height.

At the same time, the caution with which the elephant is supposed to approach insecure ground and places of doubtful[1] solidity, appears to me, so far as my own observation and experience extend, to be exaggerated, and the number of temporary bridges which are annually broken down by elephants in all parts of Ceylon, is sufficient to show that, although in captivity, and when familiar with such structures, the tame ones may, and doubtless do, exhibit all the wariness attributed to them; yet, in a state of liberty, and whilst unaccustomed to such artificial appliances, their instincts are not sufficient to ensure their safety. Besides, the fact is adverted to elsewhere,[2] that the chiefs of the Wanny, during the

[1] "One of the strongest instincts which the elephant possesses, is this which impels him to experiment upon the solidity of every surface which he is required to cross."—*Menageries, etc.* "The Elephant," vol. i. pp. 17, 19, 66.

[2] WOLF'S *Life and Adventures*, p. 151.

sovereignty of the Dutch, were accustomed to take in pitfalls the elephants which they rendered as tribute to Government.

A fact illustrative at once of the caution and the spirit of curiosity with which an elephant regards an unaccustomed object has been frequently mentioned to me by the officers engaged in opening roads through the forest. On such occasions the wooden "tracing pegs" which they drive into the ground to mark the levels taken during the day, will often be withdrawn by the elephants during the night, to such an extent as frequently to render it necessary to go over the work a second time, in order to replace them.[1]

Colonel HARDY, formerly Deputy Quarter-Master-General in Ceylon, when proceeding, about the year 1820, to a military out-post in the south-east of the island, imprudently landed in an uninhabited part of the coast, intending to take a short cut through the forest, to his destination. He both miscalculated distance and time, and, on the approach of nightfall, he was chased by a vicious rogue elephant. The pursuer was close upon him, when, to gain time, he flung down a dressing-case, which he happened to be carrying. The device was successful; the elephant halted, broke it open, and minutely examined its contents, and thus gave the colonel time to effect his escape.[2]

[1] *Private Letter* from Dr. DAVY, author of *An Account of the Interior of Ceylon.*

[2] The *Colombo Observer* for March 1858, contains an offer of a reward of twenty-five guineas for the destruction of an elephant which infested the Raja-wallé coffee plantation, in the vicinity of Kandy. Its object seemed to be less the search for food, than the satisfying of its curiosity and the gratification of its passion for mischief. Mr. TYTLER,

As regards the general sagacity of the elephant, although it has not been over-rated in the instances of those whose powers have been largely developed in captivity, an undue estimate has been formed in relation to them whilst still untamed. The difference of instincts and habits renders it difficult to institute a just comparison between them and other animals. CUVIER[1] is disposed to ascribe the exalted idea that prevails of their intellect to the feats which an elephant performs with that unique instrument, its trunk, combined with an imposing expression of countenance: but he records his own conviction that in sagacity it in no way excels the dog, and some other species of Carnivora. If there be a superiority, I am disposed to award it to the dog, not from any excess of natural capacity, but from the higher degree of development consequent on his more intimate domestication and association with man. COLERIDGE has remarked that "the ant and the bee seem to come nearer to man in understanding, and in the faculty of adapting means to proximate ends."[2]

One remarkable fact was called to my attention by a gentleman who resided on a coffee plantation at Rassawé, one of the loftiest mountains of the Ambogammoa range. More than once during the terrific thunder-bursts that precede the rains at the change of each monsoon, he ob-

the proprietor, states that it frequented the jungle near the estate, whence it was its custom to sally forth at night for the pleasure of pulling down buildings and trees, "and it seemed to have taken a spite at the pipes of the water-works; the pillars of which it several times broke down—its latest fancy being to wrench off the taps." This elephant has since been shot.

[1] CUVIER, *Règne Animal.* "Les Mammifères," p. 280.

[2] *Table Talk*, p. 63.

served that the elephants in the adjoining forest hastened from under cover of the trees and took up their station in the open ground, where I saw them on one of these occasions collected into a group; and here, he said, it was their custom to remain till the lightning had ceased, when they retired again into the jungle.[1] It must be observed, however, that showers, and especially light drizzling rain, are believed to bring the elephants from the jungle towards pathways or other openings in the forest;—and hence, in places infested by them, timid persons are afraid to travel in the afternoon during uncertain weather.

When free in its native woods the elephant evinces rather simplicity than sagacity, and its intelligence seldom exhibits itself in cunning. The rich profusion in which nature has supplied its food, and anticipated its every want, has made it independent of those devices by which carnivorous animals provide for their subsistence; and, from the absence of all rivalry between it and the other denizens of the plains, it is never required to resort to artifice for self-protection. For these reasons, in its tranquil and harmless life, it may appear to casual observers to exhibit even less than ordinary ability; but when danger and apprehension call for the exertion of its powers, those who have witnessed their display are seldom inclined to undervalue its sagacity.

[1] The elephant is believed by the Singhalese to express his uneasiness by his voice, on the approach of *rain*; and the Tamils have a proverb,—"*Listen to the elephant, rain is coming.*"

Mr. CRIPPS has related to me an instance in which a recently captured elephant was either rendered senseless from fear, or, as the native attendants asserted, *feigned death* in order to regain its freedom. It was led from the corral as usual between two tame ones, and had already proceeded far towards its destination; when, night closing in, and the torches being lighted, it refused to go on, and finally sank to the ground, apparently lifeless. Mr. CRIPPS ordered the fastenings to be removed from its legs, and when all attempts to raise it had failed, so convinced was he that it was dead, that he ordered the ropes to be taken off and the carcase abandoned. While this was being done he and a gentleman by whom he was accompanied leaned against the body to rest. They had scarcely taken their departure and proceeded a few yards, when, to their astonishment, the elephant rose with the utmost alacrity, and fled towards the jungle, screaming at the top of its voice, its cries being audible long after it had disappeared in the shades of the forest.

APPENDIX TO CHAPTER II.

NARRATIVES OF THE NATIVES OF CEYLON RELATIVE TO ENCOUNTERS WITH ROGUE ELEPHANTS.

THE following narratives have been taken down by a Singhalese gentleman, from the statements of the natives by whom they are recounted;—and they are here inserted, in order to show the opinion prevalent amongst the people of Ceylon as to the habits and propensities of the rogue elephant. The stories are given in words of my correspondent, who writes in English, as follows:—

1. "We," said my informant, who was a native trader of Caltura, "were on our way to Badulla, by way of Ratnapoora and Balangodde, to barter our merchandise for coffee. There were six in our party, myself, my brother-in-law, and four coolies, who carried on pingoes [1] our merchandise, which consisted of cloth and brass articles. About 4 o'clock, P.M., we were close to Idalgasinna, and our coolies were rather unwilling to go further for fear of elephants, which they said were sure to be met with at that noted place, especially as there had been a slight drizzling of rain during the whole afternoon. I was as much afraid of elephants as the coolies themselves; but I was anxious

[1] Yokes borne on the shoulder with a package at each end.

to proceed, and so, after a few words of encouragement addressed to them, and a prayer or two offered up to *Saman dewiyo*,[1] we resumed our journey. I also took the further precaution of hanging up a few leaves.[2] As the rain was coming down fast and thick, and I was anxious to get to our halting-place before night, we moved on at a rapid pace. My brother-in-law was in the van of the party, I myself was in the rear, and the four coolies between us, all moving along on a rugged, rocky, and difficult path ; as the road to Badulla till lately was on the sloping side of a hill, covered with jungle, pieces of projecting rock, and brushwood. It was about five o'clock in the evening, or a little later, and we had hardly cleared the foot of the hill and got to the plain below, when a rustling of leaves and a crackling of dry brushwood were heard on our right, followed immediately by the trumpeting of a *hora allia*,[3] which was making towards us. We all fled, followed by the elephant. I, who was in the rear of the party, was the first to take to flight; the coolies threw away their pingoes, and my brother-in-law his umbrella, and all ran in different directions. I hid myself behind a large boulder of granite nearly covered by jungle: but as my place of concealment was on high ground, I could see all that was going on below. The first thing I observed was the elephant returning to the place where one of the pingoes was lying: he was carrying one of the coolies in a coil of his trunk. The body of the man was dangling with the head downward. I cannot say whether he was then alive or not ; I could not perceive any marks of

[1] The tutelary spirit of the sacred mountain, Adam's Peak.

[2] The Singhalese hold the belief, that twigs taken from one bush and placed on another growing close to a pathway, ensure protection to travellers from the attacks of wild animals, and especially of elephants. Can it be that the latter avoid the path, on discovering this evidence of the proximity of recent passengers?

[3] A rogue elephant.

blood or bruises on his person: but he appeared to be lifeless. The elephant placed him down on the ground, put the pingo on his (the man's) shoulder, steadying both the man and the pingo with his trunk and fore legs. But the man of course did not move or stand up with his pingo. Seeing this, the elephant again raised the cooly and dashed him against the ground, and then trampled the body to a very jelly. This done, he took up the pingo and moved away from the spot; but at the distance of about a fathom or two, laid it down again, and ripping open one of the bundles, took out of it all the contents, *somans*,[1] *cambāyas*,[2] handkerchiefs, and several pieces of white cambrick cloth, all which he tore to small pieces, and flung them wildly here and there. He did the same with all the other pingoes. When this was over the elephant quietly walked away into the jungle, trumpeting all the way as far as I could hear. When danger was past I came out of my concealment, and returned to the place where we had halted that morning. Here the rest of my companions joined me soon after. The next morning we set out again on our journey, our party being now increased by some seven or eight traders from Salpity Corle: but this time we did not meet with the elephant. We found the mangled corpse of our cooly on the same spot where I had seen it the day before, together with the torn pieces of my cloths, of which we collected as fast as we could the few which were serviceable, and all the brass utensils which were quite uninjured. That elephant was a noted rogue. He had before this killed many people on that road, especially those carrying pingoes of coco-nut oil and ghee. He was afterwards killed by an Englishman. The incidents I have mentioned above, took place about twenty years ago."

[1] Woman's robe. [2] The figured cloth worn by men.

The following also relates to the same locality. It was narrated to me by an old Moorman of Barberyn, who, during his earlier years, led the life of a pedlar.

2. "I and another," said he, "were on our way to Badulla, one day some twenty-five or thirty years ago. We were quietly moving along a path which wound round a hill, when all of a sudden, and without the slightest previous intimation either by the rustling of leaves or by any other sign, a huge elephant with short tusks rushed to the path. Where he had been before I can't say; I believe he must have been lying in wait for travellers. In a moment he rushed forward to the road, trumpeting dreadfully, and seized my companion. I, who happened to be in the rear, took to flight, pursued by the elephant, which had already killed my companion by striking him against the ground. I had not moved more than seven or eight fathoms, when the elephant seized me, and threw me up with such force, that I was carried high into the air towards a *Cahata* tree, whose branches caught me and prevented my falling to the ground. By this I received no other injury than the dislocation of one of my wrists. I do not know whether the elephant saw me after he had hurled me away through the air; but certainly he did not come to the tree to which I was then clinging: even if he had come, he couldn't have done me any more harm, as the branch on which I was was far beyond the reach of his trunk, and the tree itself too large for him to pull down. The next thing I saw was the elephant returning to the corpse of my companion, which he again threw on the ground, and placing one of his fore-feet on it, he tore it with his trunk limb after limb; and dabbled in the blood that flowed from the shapeless mass of flesh which he was still holding under his foot."

3. "In 1847 or '46," said another informant, "I was a

superintendent of a coco-nut estate belonging to Mr. Armitage, situated about twelve miles from Negombo. A rogue elephant did considerable injury to the estate at that time; and one day, hearing that it was then on the plantation, a Mr. Lindsay, an Englishman, who was proprietor of the adjoining property, and myself, accompanied by some seven or eight people of the neighbouring village, went out, carrying with us six rifles loaded and primed. We continued to walk along a path which, near one of its turns, had some bushes on one side. We had calculated to come up with the brute where it had been seen half an hour before; but no sooner had one of our men, who was walking foremost, seen the animal at the distance of some fifteen or twenty fathoms, than he exclaimed, 'There! there!' and immediately took to his heels, and we all followed his example. The elephant did not see us until we had run some fifteen or twenty paces from the spot where we turned, when he gave us chase, screaming frightfully as he came on. The Englishman managed to climb a tree, and the rest of my companions did the same; as for myself I could not, although I made one or two superhuman efforts. But there was no time to be lost. The elephant was running at me with his trunk bent down in a curve towards the ground. At this critical moment Mr. Lindsay held out his foot to me, with the help of which and then of the branches of the tree, which were three or four feet above my head, I managed to scramble up to a branch. The elephant came directly to the tree and attempted to force it down, which he could not. He first coiled his trunk round the stem, and pulled it with all his might, but with no effect. He then applied his head to the tree, and pushed for several minutes, but with no better success. He then trampled with his feet all the projecting roots, moving, as he did so, several times round and round the tree. Lastly, failing in all this, and seeing a pile of timber, which I had lately cut, at a short distance from us, he removed it all (thirty-six pieces) one at a time to the root of the tree, and piled them up in a regular business-like manner; then placing his hind feet on this pile, he raised the fore part of his body, and reached out his trunk, but still he could not touch us, as we were too far above him. The Englishman then fired, and the ball took effect somewhere on the elephant's head, but did not kill him. It made him only the more furious. The next shot, however, levelled him to the ground. I afterwards brought the skull of the animal to Colombo, and it is still to be seen at the house of Mr. Armitage."

4. "One night a herd of elephants entered a village in the Four Corles. After doing considerable injury to plaintain bushes and young coco-nut trees, they retired, the villagers being unable to do anything to protect their fruit trees from destruction. But one elephant was left behind, who continued to scream the whole night through at the same spot. It was then discovered that the elephant, on seeing a jak fruit on a tree somewhat beyond the reach of his trunk, had raised himself on his hind legs, placing his fore feet against the stem, in order to lay hold of the fruit, but unluckily for him there happened to be another tree standing so close to it that the vacant space between the two stems was only a few inches. During his attempts to take hold of the fruit one of his legs happened to get in between the two trees, where, on account of his weight and his clumsy attempts to extricate himself, it got so firmly wedged that he could not remove it, and in this awkward position he remained for some days, till he died on the spot."

CHAPTER III.

ELEPHANT SHOOTING.

As the shooting of an elephant, whatever endurance and adroitness the sport may display in other respects, requires the smallest possible skill as a marksman, the numbers which are annually slain in this way may be regarded less as a test of the expertness of the sportsman, than as evidence of the multitudes of elephants abounding in those parts of Ceylon to which they resort. One officer, Major ROGERS, killed upwards of 1,400; another, Captain GALLWEY, has the credit of slaying more than half that number; Major SKINNER, the Commissioner of Roads, almost as many; and less persevering aspirants follow at humbler distances.[1]

[1] To persons like myself, who are not addicted to what is called "sport," the statement of these wholesale slaughters is calculated to excite surprise and curiosity as to the nature of a passion that impels men to self exposure and privation, in a pursuit which presents nothing but the monotonous recurrence of scenes of blood and suffering. Sir S. BAKER, who has recently published, under the title of "*The Rifle and the Hound in Ceylon*," an account of his exploits in the forest, gives us the assurance that "*all real sportsmen are tender-hearted men, who shun cruelty to an animal, and are easily moved by a tale of distress;*" and that although man is naturally bloodthirsty, and a beast of prey by instinct, yet that the true sportsman is distinguished from the rest of the human race by his "*love of nature and of noble scenery.*" In support of this pretension to a gentler nature than the rest of mankind, the author proceeds to attest his own abhorrence of cruelty by nar-

But notwithstanding this prodigious destruction, a reward of a few shillings per head offered by the Government for taking elephants was claimed for 3,500 destroyed in part of the northern province alone, in less than three years prior to 1848; and between 1851 and 1856, a similar reward was paid for 2,000 in the southern province, between Galle and Hambangtotte.

Although there is little opportunity in an elephant battue for the display of proficiency as a shot there is one feature in the sport, as conducted in Ceylon, which

rating the sufferings of an old hound, which, although "toothless," he cheered on to assail a boar at bay, but the poor dog recoiled "covered with blood, cut nearly in half, with a wound fourteen inches in length, from the lower part of the belly, passing up the flank, completely severing the muscles of the hind leg, and extending up the spine; his hind leg having the appearance of being nearly off." In this state, forgetful of the character he had so lately given of the true sportsman, as a lover of nature and a hater of cruelty, he encouraged "the poor old dog," as he calls him, to resume the fight with the boar, which lasted for an hour, when he managed to call the dogs off; and, perfectly exhausted, the mangled hound crawled out of the jungle with several additional wounds, including a severe gash in his throat. "He fell from exhaustion, and we made a litter with two poles and a horsecloth to carry him home." (P. 314.) If such were the habitual enjoyments of this class of sportsmen, their motiveless massacres would admit of no manly justification. In comparison with them one is disposed to regard almost with favour the exploits of a hunter like Major ROGERS, who is said to have applied the value of the ivory obtained from his encounters towards the purchase of his successive regimental commissions, and had, therefore, an object, however disproportionate, in his slaughter of 1,400 elephants.

One gentleman in Ceylon, not less distinguished for his genuine kindness of heart, than for his marvellous success in shooting elephants, avowed to me that the eagerness with which he found himself impelled to pursue them had often excited surprise in his own mind; and although he had never read the theory of Lord Kames, or the speculations of Vicesimus Knox, he had come to the conclusion that the passion thus excited within him was a remnant of the hunter's instinct, with which man was originally endowed to enable him, by the chase, to support existence in a state of nature, and which, though rendered dormant by civilisation, had not been utterly eradicated.

This theory is at least more consistent and intelligible than the "love of nature and scenery," sentimentally propounded by the author quoted above.

contrasts favourably with the slaughterhouse details chronicled with revolting minuteness in some recent accounts of elephant shooting in South Africa. The practice in Ceylon is to aim invariably at the head, and the sportsman finds his safety to consist in boldly facing the animal, advancing to within fifteen paces, and lodging a bullet, either in the temple or in the hollow over the eye, or in a well-known spot immediately above the trunk, where the weaker structure of the skull affords an easy access to the brain.[1] The region of the ear is also a fatal spot, and often resorted to,—the places I have mentioned in the front of the head being only accessible when the animal is "charging." Professor HARRISON, in his communication to the Royal Irish Academy on the Anatomy of the Elephant, has rendered an intelligible explanation of this in the following passage descriptive of the cranium:—"It exhibits two remarkable facts: *first*, the small space occupied by the brain; and, *secondly*, the beautiful and curious structure of the bones of the head. The two tables of all these bones, except the occipital, are separated by rows of large cells, some from four to five inches in length, others only small, irregular, and honey-comb-like:—these all communicate with each other, and, through the frontal sinuses, with

[1] The vulnerability of the elephant in this region of the head was known to the ancients, and PLINY, describing a combat of elephants in the amphitheatre at Rome, says, that one was slain by a single blow, "pilum sub oculo adactum, in vitalia capitis venerat." (Lib. viii. c. 7.) Notwithstanding the comparative facility of access to the brain afforded at this spot, an ordinary leaden bullet is not certain to penetrate, and frequently becomes flattened. The hunters, to counteract this, are accustomed to harden the ball, by the introduction of a small portion of type-metal along with the lead.

the cavity of the nose, and also with the tympanum or drum of each ear; consequently, as in some birds, these cells are filled with air, and thus while the skull attains a great size in order to afford an extensive surface for the attachment of muscles, and a mechanical support for the tusks, it is at the same time very light and

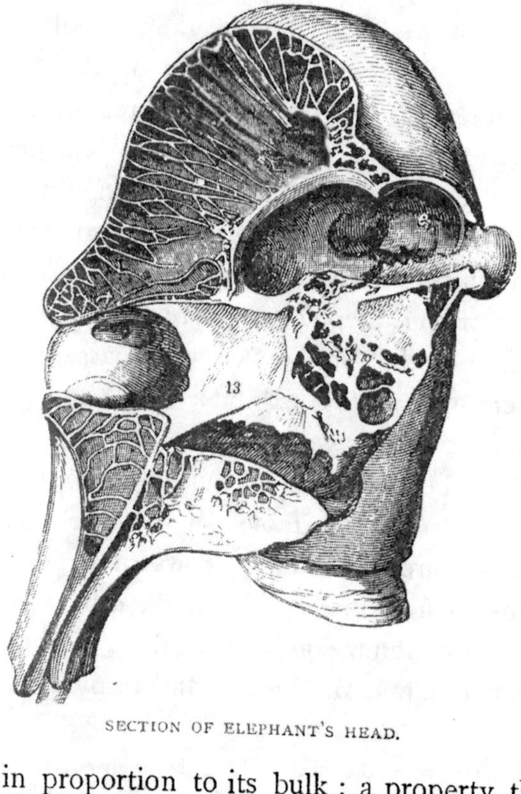

SECTION OF ELEPHANT'S HEAD.

buoyant in proportion to its bulk; a property the more valuable as the animal is fond of water and bathes in deep rivers."

Generally speaking, as regards the elephants of Ceylon, a single ball, planted in the forehead, ends the existence of the noble creature instantaneously: and expert sportsmen have been known to kill right and left, one with each barrel; but occasionally an elephant will not fall before several shots have been lodged in his head. But as regards the African elephant, Sir S. Baker, the explorer of the Nile, than whom no one has had greater experience of elephant shooting in both countries, is of opinion that, owing to a peculiar configuration of the head, it is next to impossible to kill by a front shot.[1]

Contrasted with this, one reads with a shudder the sickening details of the African huntsman approaching *behind* the retiring animal, and of the torture inflicted by the shower of bullets which tear up its flesh and lacerate its flank and shoulders.[2]

[1] "The head is so peculiarly formed that the ball either passes over the brain, or lodges in the immensely solid bones and cartilages that contain the roots of the tusks . . . . . . The brain of the African species, he says, rests upon a plate of bone exactly above the roots of the upper grinders and is thus wonderfully protected from a front shot, as it lies so low that the ball passes over it when the elephant raises his head, which he invariably does when in anger, until close to the object of his attack. . . . . I had always held the opinion that the African elephant might be killed with the same facility as that of Ceylon *by a forehead shot;* but I have found by much experience that I was entirely wrong and that although by chance an African elephant may be killed by the front shot, it is the exception to the rule." (*The Albert Nyanza,* vol. i. p. 277.)

[2] In Mr. Gordon Cumming's account of a *Hunter's Life in South Africa,* there is a narrative of his pursuit of a unded elephant which he had lamed by lodging a ball in its shoulder-blade. It limped slowly towards a tree, against which it leaned itself in helpless agony, whilst its pursuer seated himself in front of it, in safety, to *boil his coffee,* and observe its sufferings. The story is continued as follows:—"Having admired him for a considerable time, *I resolved to make experiments on vulnerable points;* and approaching very near I fired several bullets at different parts of his enormous skull. He only acknowledged the shots by a salaam-like movement of his trunk, with the point of which he gently touched the wounds with a striking and peculiar action. Surprised and shocked at finding that I was only prolonging the sufferings of the noble beast, which bore its trials with such dignified composure, I resolved to finish the proceeding with all possible despatch, and accordingly opened fire upon him from the left side, aiming at the shoulder. I first fired *six* shots with the two-grooved rifle, which must have eventually proved mortal. After which I fired *six* shots

The shooting of elephants in Ceylon has been described with tiresome iteration in the successive journals of sporting gentlemen, but one who turns to their pages for natural traits of the animal and his instincts is disappointed to find little beyond graphic sketches of the daring and exploits of his pursuers, most of whom, having had no further opportunity of observation than is derived from a casual encounter with the outraged animal, have apparently tried to exalt their own prowess by misrepresenting the ordinary character of the elephant, describing it as "savage, wary, and revengeful."[1]

These epithets may undoubtedly apply to the outcasts from the herd, the "rogues" or *hora allia*, but so small is the proportion of these that there is not probably more than one *rogue* to be found for every five hundred of

at the same part with the Dutch six-pounder. *Large tears now trickled from his eyes, which he slowly shut and opened, his colossal frame shivered convulsively, and falling on his side, he expired.*" (Vol. ii. p. 10.)

In another place, after detailing the manner in which he assailed a poor animal, he says: "I was loading and firing as fast as could be, sometimes at the head, sometimes behind the shoulder, until my elephant's fore-quarter was a mass of gore; notwithstanding which he continued to hold on, leaving the grass and branches of the forest scarlet in his wake. . . . . . Having fired *thirty-five rounds* with my two-grooved rifle, I opened upon him with the Dutch six-pounder, and when forty bullets had perforated his hide, he began for the first time to evince signs of a dilapidated constitution." The disgusting description is closed thus: "Throughout the charge he repeatedly cooled his person with large quantities of water, which he ejected from his trunk over his sides and back, and just as the pangs of death came over him, he stood trembling violently beside a thorn tree, and kept pouring water into his bloody mouth until he died, when he pitched heavily forward with the whole weight of his fore-quarters resting on the points of his tusks. The strain was fair, and the tusks did not yield; but the portion of his head in which the tusks were embedded, extending a long way above the eye, yielded and burst with a muffled crash." (*Ib.* vol. ii. pp. 4, 5.)

[1] *The Rifle and the Hound in Ceylon;* by Sir S. BAKER, pp. 8, 9. "Next to a rogue in ferocity, and even more persevering in the pursuit of her victim, is a female elephant." But he appends the significant qualification, "*when her young one has been killed.*" (*Ibid.* p. 13.)

those in herds; and it is a manifest error, arising from imperfect information, to extend this censure to elephants generally, or to suppose it to be an animal "thirsting for blood, lying in wait in the jungle to rush on the unwary passer-by, and knowing no greater pleasure than the act of crushing his victim to a shapeless mass beneath his feet."[1] The cruelties practised by hunters have no doubt taught these sagacious creatures to be cautious and alert, but their precautions are simply defensive; and beyond the alarm and apprehension which they evince on the approach of man, they exhibit no indication of hostility or thirst for blood.

An ordinary traveller seldom comes upon elephants unless after sunset or towards daybreak, as they go to or return from their nightly visits to the tanks: but when by accident a herd is disturbed by day, they evince, if unattacked, no disposition to become assailants; and if the attitude of defence which they instinctively assume prove sufficient to check the approach of the intruder, no further demonstration is to be apprehended.

Even the hunters who go in search of them find them in positions and occupations altogether inconsistent with the idea of their being savage, wary, or revengeful. Their demeanour when undisturbed is indicative of gentleness and timidity, and their actions bespeak lassitude and indolence, induced not alone by heat, but probably ascribable in some degree to the fact that the night has been spent in watchfulness and amusement. A few are generally browsing listlessly on the trees and

[1] *The Rifle and the Hound*, p. 13.

plants within reach, others fanning themselves with leafy branches, and a few are asleep; whilst the young run playfully among the herd, the emblems of innocence, as the older ones are of peacefulness and gravity.

Almost every elephant may be observed to exhibit some peculiar action of the limbs when standing at rest; some move the head monotonously in a circle, or from right to left; some swing their feet back and forward; others flap their ears or sway themselves from side to side, or rise and sink by alternately bending and straightening the fore knees. As the opportunities of observing this custom have been almost confined to elephants in captivity, it has been conjectured to arise from some morbid habit contracted during the length of a voyage by sea,[1] or from an instinctive impulse to substitute an artificial motion in lieu of their wonted exercise; but this supposition is erroneous; the propensity being equally displayed by those at liberty and those in captivity. When surprised by sportsmen in the depths of the jungle, individuals of a herd are always to be seen occupied in swinging their limbs in this manner; and in the corrals which I have seen, where whole herds have been captured, the elephants, in the midst of the utmost excitement, and even after the most vigorous charges, if they halted for a moment in stupor and exhaustion, manifested their wonted habit, and swung their limbs or swayed their bodies to and fro incessantly. So far from its being a substitute for exercise, those in the Government employment in Ceylon are observed to practise their acquired

[1] *Menageries etc.* "The Elephant," ch. i. p. 21.

motion, whatever it may be, with increased vigour when thoroughly fatigued after excessive work. Even the favourite practice of fanning themselves with a leafy branch seems less an enjoyment in itself than a resource when listless and at rest. The term "fidgetty" seems to describe appropriately the temperament of the elephant.

They evince the strongest love of retirement and a corresponding dislike to intrusion. The approach of a stranger is perceived less by the eye, the quickness of which is not remarkable (besides which its range is obscured by the foliage), than by sensitive smell and singular acuteness of hearing; and the whole herd is put in instant but noiseless motion towards some deeper and more secure retreat. The effectual manner in which an animal of the prodigious size of the elephant can conceal himself, and the motionless silence which he preserves, is quite surprising; whilst beaters pass and repass within a few yards of his hiding place, he will maintain his ground till the hunter, creeping almost close to his legs, sees his little eye peering out through the leaves, when, finding himself discovered, the elephant breaks away with a crash, levelling the brushwood in his headlong career.

If surprised in open ground, where stealthy retreat is impracticable, a herd will hesitate in indecision, and, after a few meaningless movements, stand huddled together in a group, whilst one or two, more adventurous than the rest, advance a few steps to reconnoitre. Elephants are generally observed to be bolder in open ground than in cover, but, if bold at all, far more dangerous in cover than in open ground.

In searching for them, sportsmen often avail themselves of the expertness of the native trackers; and notwithstanding the demonstration of Combe that the brain of the timid Singhalese is deficient in the organ of destructiveness,[1] he shows an instinct for hunting, and exhibits in the pursuit of the elephant a courage and adroitness far surpassing in interest the mere handling of the rifle, which is the principal share of the proceeding that falls to his European companions.

The beater on these occasions has the double task of finding the game and carrying the guns; and, in an animated communication to me, an experienced sportsman describes "this light and active creature, with his long glossy hair hanging down his shoulders, every muscle quivering with excitement; and his countenance lighting up with intense animation, leaping from rock to rock, as nimble as a chamois, tracking the gigantic game like a blood-hound, falling behind as he comes up with it, and as the elephants, baffled and irritated, make the first stand, passing one rifle into your eager hand and holding the other ready whilst right and left each barrel performs its mission, and if fortune does not flag, and the second gun is as successful as the first, three or four huge carcases are piled one on another within a space equal to the area of a dining room."[2]

It is curious that in these encounters the herd never

[1] *System of Phrenology*, by GEO. COMBE, vol. i. p. 256.

[2] Private letter from Capt. PHILIP PAYNE GALLWEY.

rush forward in a body, as buffaloes or bisons do, but only one elephant at a time moves in advance of the rest to confront, or, as it is called, to "charge," the assailants. I have heard of but one instance in which *two* so advanced as champions of their companions. Sometimes, indeed, the whole herd will follow a leader, and manœuvre in his rear like a body of cavalry; but so large a party are necessarily liable to panic; and, one of them having turned in alarm, the entire body retreat with terrified precipitation.

As regards boldness and courage, a strange variety of temperament is observable amongst elephants, but it may be affirmed that they are much more generally timid than courageous. One herd may be as difficult to approach as deer, gliding away through the jungle so gently and quickly that scarcely a trace marks their passage; another, in apparent stupor, will huddle themselves together like swine, and allow their assailant to come within a few yards before they break away in terror; and a third will await his approach without motion, and then advance with fury to the "charge."

In individuals the same differences are discernible; one flies on the first appearance of danger, whilst another, alone and unsupported, will face a whole host of enemies. When wounded and infuriated with pain, many of them become literally savage;[1] but, so unaccustomed are they to act as assailants, and so awkward

[1] Some years ago an elephant which had been wounded by a native, near Hambangtotte, pursued the man into the town, followed him along the street, trampled him to death in the bazaar before a crowd of terrified spectators, and succeeded in making good its retreat to the jungle.

and inexpert in using their strength, that they rarely or ever succeed in killing a pursuer who falls into their power. Although the pressure of a foot, a blow with the trunk, or a thrust with the tusk, could scarcely fail to prove fatal, three-fourths of those so overtaken have escaped without serious injury. So great is this chance of impunity, that the sportsman prefers to approach within about fifteen paces of the advancing elephant, a space which gives time for a second fire should the first shot prove ineffectual, and should both fail there is still opportunity for flight.

Amongst full-grown timber, a skilful runner can escape from an elephant by "dodging" round the trees, but in cleared land, and low brushwood, the difficulty is much increased, as the small growth of underwood which obstructs the movements of man presents no obstacle to those of an elephant. On the other hand, on level and open ground the chances are rather in favour of the elephant, as his pace in full flight exceeds that of man, although as a general rule, it is unequal to that of a horse, as has been sometimes asserted.[1]

The incessant slaughter of elephants by sportsmen in Ceylon, appears to be merely in subordination to the influence of the organ of destructiveness, since the carcase is never applied to any useful purpose, but left to decompose and to defile the air of the forest. The flesh is occasionally tasted as a matter of curiosity: as a steak it is coarse and tough; but the tongue is as delicate as

[1] SHAW, in his *Zoology*, asserts that an elephant can run as swiftly as a horse can gallop. London, 1800–6, vol. i. p. 216.

that of an ox; and the foot is said to make palatable soup. The Caffres attached to the pioneer corps in the Kandyan province are in the habit of securing the heart of any elephant shot in their vicinity, and say it is their custom to eat it in Africa. The hide it has been found impracticable to tan in Ceylon, or to convert to any useful purpose, but the bones of those shot have of late years been collected and used for manuring coffee estates. The hair of the tail, which is extremely strong and horny, is mounted by the native goldsmith, and made into bracelets; and the teeth are sawn by the Moormen at Galle (as they used to be by the Romans during a scarcity of ivory) into plates, out of which they fashion numerous articles of ornament, knife-handles, card racks, and "presse-papiers."

NOTE.

AMONGST extraordinary recoveries from desperate wounds, I venture to record here an instance which occurred in Ceylon to a gentleman while engaged in the chase of elephants, and which, I apprehend, has few parallels in pathological experience. Lieutenant GERARD FRETZ, of the Ceylon Rifle Regiment, whilst firing at an elephant in the vicinity of Fort MacDonald, in Ouvah, was wounded in the face by the bursting of his fowling-piece, on the 22nd January, 1828. He was then about thirty-two years of age. On raising him, it was found that part of the breech of the gun and about two inches of the barrel had been driven through the frontal sinus at the junction of the nose and forehead. It had sunk almost perpendicularly till the iron plate called "the tail-pin," by which the barrel is made fast to the stock by a screw, had descended through the palate, carrying with it the screw, one extremity of which had forced itself into the right nostril, where it was discernible externally, whilst the headed end lay in contact with his tongue. To extract the jagged mass of iron thus sunk in the ethmoidal and sphenoidal cells was found hopelessly impracticable; but strange to tell, after the inflammation subsided, Mr. FRETZ recovered rapidly; his general health was unimpaired, and he returned to his regiment with this singular appendage firmly embedded behind the bones of his face. He took his turn of duty as usual, attained the command of his company, participated in all the enjoyments of the mess-room, and died *eight years afterwards*, on the 1st of April, 1836, not from any consequences of this fearful wound, but from fever and inflammation brought on by other causes.

So little was he apparently inconvenienced by the presence of the strange body in his palate that he was accustomed with his finger partially to undo the screw, which but for its extreme length he might altogether have withdrawn. To enable this to be done, and possibly to assist by this means the extraction of the breech itself through the original orifice (which never entirely closed), an attempt was made in 1835 to take off a portion of the screw with a file; but, after having cut it three parts through the operation was interrupted, chiefly owing to the carelessness and indifference of Capt. FRETZ, whose death occurred before the attempt could be resumed. The piece of iron, on being removed after his decease, was found to measure 2¾ inches in length, and weighed two scruples more than two ounces and three quarters. A cast of the breech and screw now forms No. 2790 amongst the deposits in the Medical Museum of Chatham.

PART II.

MODE OF CAPTURE.

CHAPTER I.

AN ELEPHANT CORRAL.

So long as the elephants of Ceylon were merely required in small numbers for the pageantry of the native princes, or the sacred processions of the Buddhist temples, their capture was effected either by the instrumentality of female decoys, or by the artifices and agility of the individuals and castes who devoted themselves to their pursuit and training. But after the arrival of the European conquerors of the island, and when it had become expedient to take advantage of the strength and intelligence of these creatures in clearing forests and constructing roads and other works, establishments were organised on a great scale by the Portuguese and Dutch, and the supply of elephants kept up by periodical battues conducted at the cost of the Government, on a plan similar to that adopted on the continent of India, when herds varying in number from twenty to one hundred and upwards are driven into concealed enclosures and secured.

In both these processes, success is entirely dependent on the skill with which the captors turn to advantage the panic and inexperience of the wild elephant, since all attempts would be futile to subdue or confine by ordinary force an animal of such strength and sagacity.[1]

KNOX describes with circumstantiality the mode adopted, two centuries ago, by the servants of the King of Kandy to catch elephants for the royal stud. He says, "After discovering the retreat of such as have tusks, unto these they drive some *she elephants*, which they bring with them for the purpose, which, when once the males have got a sight of, they will never leave, but follow them wheresoever they go; and the females are so used to it that they will do whatsoever, either by word or a beck, their keepers bid them. And so they delude them along through towns and countries, and through the streets of the city, even to the very gates of the king's palace, where sometimes they seize upon them by snares,

[1] The device of taking them by means of pitfalls still prevails in India; but in addition to the difficulty of providing against that caution with which the elephant is supposed to reconnoitre suspicious ground, it has the further disadvantage of exposing him to injury from bruises and dislocations in his fall. Still it was the mode of capture employed by the Singhalese, and so late as 1750 WOLF relates that the native chiefs of the Wanny, when capturing elephants for the Dutch, made "pits some fathoms deep in those places whither the elephant is wont to go in search of food, across which were laid poles covered with branches and baited with the food of which he is fondest, making towards which he finds himself taken unawares. Thereafter being subdued by fright and exhaustion, he was assisted to raise himself to the surface by means of hurdles and earth, which he placed underfoot as they were thrown down to him, till he was enabled to step out on solid ground, when the noosers and decoys were in readiness to tie him up to the nearest tree." (See WOLF's *Life and Adventures*, p. 152.) Shakspeare appears to have been acquainted with the plan of taking elephants in pitfalls: Decius, encouraging the conspirators, reminds them of Cæsar's taste for anecdotes of animals, by which he would undertake to lure him to his fate:

"For he loves to hear
That unicorns may be betrayed with trees,
And bears with glasses: *elephants with holes.*"

JULIUS CÆSAR, Act ii. Scene I.

and sometimes by driving them into a kind of pound, they catch them."[1]

In Nepaul and Burmah, and throughout the Chin-Indian Peninsula, when in pursuit of single elephants, either *rogues* detached from the herd, or individuals who have been marked for the beauty of their ivory, the natives avail themselves of the aid of females in order to effect their approaches and secure an opportunity of casting a noose over the foot of the destined captive. All accounts concur in expressing high admiration of their courage and address; but from what has fallen under my own observation, added to the descriptions I have heard from other eye-witnesses, I am inclined to believe that in such exploits the Moormen of Ceylon evince a daring and adroitness, surpassing all others.

These professional elephant catchers, or, as they are called, Panickeas, inhabit the Moorish villages in the north and north-east of the island, and from time immemorial have been engaged in taking elephants, which are afterwards trained by Arabs, chiefly for the use of the rajahs and native princes in the south of India, whose vakeels are periodically despatched to make purchases in Ceylon.

The ability evinced by these men in tracing elephants through the woods has almost the certainty of instinct; and hence their services are eagerly sought by the European sportsmen who go down into their country in search of game. So keen is their glance, that like hounds running "breast high" they will follow the course of an

[1] Knox's *Historical Relation of Ceylon*, A.D. 1681, part i. ch. vi. p. 21.

elephant, almost at the top of their speed, over glades covered with stunted grass, where the eye of a stranger would fail to discover a trace of its passage, and on through forests strewn with dry leaves, where it seems impossible to perceive a footstep. Here they are guided by a bent or broken twig, or by a leaf dropped from the animal's mouth, on which the pressure of a tooth may be detected. If at fault, they fetch a circuit like a setter, till lighting on some fresh marks, they go a-head again with renewed vigour. So delicate is the sense of smell in the elephant, and so indispensable is it to go against the wind in approaching him, that on those occasions when the wind is so still that its direction cannot be otherwise discerned, the Panickeas will suspend the film of a gossamer to determine it and shape their course accordingly.

They are enabled by the inspection of the footmarks, when impressed in soft clay, to describe the size as well as the number of a herd before it is seen; the height of an elephant at the shoulder being as nearly as possible twice the circumference of his fore foot.[1]

On overtaking the game their courage is as conspicuous as their sagacity. If they have confidence in the sportsman for whom they are finding, they will advance to the very heel of the elephant, slap him on the quarter, and

[1] Previous to the death of the female elephant in the Zoological Gardens, in the Regent's Park, in 1851, Mr. MITCHELL, the Secretary, caused measurements to be accurately made, and found the statement of the Singhalese hunters to be strictly correct, the height at the shoulders being precisely twice the circumference of the fore foot. In an African elephant killed by Sir S. Baker, this proportion did not hold good, as the circumference of the fore foot was 4 feet 11¼ inches, and the height at the shoulder 10 feet 6½ inches. (BAKER, *The Albert Nyanza*, vol. ii. p. 10.)

convert his timidity into anger, till he turns upon his tormentor and exposes his front to receive the bullet which awaits him.[1]

So fearless and confident are they, that two men, without aid or attendants, will boldly attempt to capture the largest-sized elephant. Their only weapon is a flexible rope made of deer's or buffalo's hide, with which it is their object to secure one of the hind legs. This they effect either by following in its footsteps when in motion or by stealing close up to it when at rest, and availing themselves of its well known propensity at such moments to swing the feet backwards and forwards, they contrive to slip a noose over the hind leg.

At other times this is achieved by spreading the noose on the ground partially concealed by roots and leaves beneath a tree on which one of the party is stationed, whose business it is to lift it suddenly by means of a cord,

[1] Major SKINNER, the Chief Officer at the head of the Commission of Roads, in Ceylon, in writing to me, mentions an anecdote illustrative of the daring of the Panickeas. "I once saw," he says, "a very beautiful example of the confidence with which these fellows, from their knowledge of the elephants, meet their worst defiance. It was in Neuera-Kalawa; I was bivouacking on the bank of a river, and had been kept out so late that I did not get to my tent until between 9 and 10 at night. On our return towards it we passed several single elephants making their way to the nearest water, but at length we came upon a large herd that had taken possession of the only road by which we could pass, and which no intimidation would induce to move off. I had some Panickeas with me; they knew the herd, and counselled extreme caution. After trying every device we could think of for a length of time, a little old Moorman of the party came to me and requested we should all retire to a distance. He then took a couple of chules (flambeaux of dried wood, or coco-nut leaves), one in each hand, and waving them above his head till they flamed out fiercely, he advanced at a deliberate pace to within a few yards of the elephant who was acting as leader of the party, and who was growling and trumpeting in his rage, and flourished the flaming torches in his face. The effect was instantaneous; the whole herd dashed away in a panic, bellowing, screaming, and crushing through the underwood, whilst we availed ourselves of the open path to make our way to our tents."

raising it on the elephant's leg at the moment when his companion has succeeded in provoking him to place his foot within the circle, the other end having been previously made fast to the stem of the tree. Should the noosing be effected in open ground, and no tree of sufficient strength be at hand round which to wind the rope, one of the Moors, allowing himself to be pursued by the enraged elephant, entices him towards the nearest grove; where his companion, dexterously laying hold of the rope as it trails along the ground, suddenly coils it round a suitable stem, and brings the fugitive to a stand-still. On finding himself thus arrested, the natural impulse of the captive is to turn on the man who is engaged in making fast the rope, a movement which it is the duty of his colleague to prevent by running up close to the elephant's head and provoking the animal to confront him by irritating gesticulations and taunting shouts of *dah! dah!* a monosyllable, the sound of which the elephant peculiarly dislikes. Meanwhile the first assailant, having secured one noose, comes up from behind with another, with which, amidst the vain rage and struggles of the victim, he entraps a fore leg, the rope being, as before, secured to another tree in front, and the whole four feet having been thus entangled, the capture is completed.

A shelter is then run up with branches, to protect the captive from the sun, and the hunters proceed to build a wigwam for themselves in front of him, kindling their fires for cooking, and making all the necessary arrangements for remaining day and night on the spot to await the process of subduing and taming his rage. In my journeys through the forest I have come unexpectedly on the halting place of adventurous hunters when thus engaged; and on one occasion, about sunrise, in ascending the steep ridge from the bed of the Malwatte river, the foremost rider of our party was suddenly driven back by the trumpeting of a furious elephant, which we found picketed by two Panickeas on the crest of the bank. In such restraint, the elephant soon ceases to struggle; and what with the exhaustion of rage and resistance, the terror of fire which he dreads, and the constant annoyance of smoke which he detests, in a very short time, a few weeks at the most, his spirit becomes subdued; then being plentifully supplied with plantains and fresh food, and indulged with water, in which he luxuriates, he grows so far reconciled to his keepers that they at length venture to remove him to their own village, and eventually to the sea-side for shipment to India.

No part of the hunter's performances exhibits greater skill and audacity than this first forced march of the recently captured elephant through the great central forests to the sea-coast. As he is still too morose to submit to be ridden, and it would be equally impossible to lead or to drive him by force, the ingenuity of the captors is displayed in alternately irritating and eluding him, but always so attracting his attention as to allure him along in the direction in which they want him to go. Some assistance is derived from the rope by which the original capture was effected, and which, as it serves to make him safe at night, is never removed from the leg till his taming is sufficiently advanced to permit of his being entrusted with partial liberty.

In Ceylon the principal place for exporting these animals to India is Manaar, on the western coast, to which the Arabs from the continent resort, bringing with them horses to be bartered for elephants. In order to reach the sea, open plains must be traversed, across which it requires the utmost courage, agility, and patience of the Moors to coax their reluctant charge. At Manaar the elephants are usually detained till any wound on the leg caused by the rope has been healed, when the shipment is effected in the most primitive manner. It being next to impossible to induce the still untamed creature to walk on board, and no mechanical contrivances being provided to ship him, a dhoney, or native boat, of about forty tons' burthen, and about three parts filled with the strong ribbed leaves of the Palmyra palm, is brought alongside the quay in front of the Old Dutch Fort, and lashed so that the gunwale may be as nearly as possible on a line with the level of the wharf. The elephant being placed with his back to the water is forced by goads to retreat till his hind legs go over the side of the quay, but the main contest commences when it is attempted to disengage his fore feet from the shore, and force him to entrust himself on board. The scene becomes exciting from the screams and trumpeting of the elephants, the shouts of the Arabs, the calls of the Moors, and the rushing of the crowd. Meanwhile the huge creature strains every nerve to regain the land; and the day is often consumed before his efforts are overcome, and he finds himself fairly afloat. The same dhoney will take from four to five elephants, who place themselves athwart it, and exhibit amusing adroitness in accommodating their movements to the rolling of the little vessel ; and in this way they are ferried across the narrow strait which separates Ceylon from the continent of India.[1]

But the feat of ensnaring and subduing a single elephant, courageous as it is, and demonstrative of the supremacy with which man wields his "dominion over every beast of the earth," falls far short of the daring exploit of capturing a whole herd : when from thirty to one hundred wild elephants are entrapped in one vast decoy. The mode of effecting this, as it is practised in Ceylon, is no doubt imitated, but with considerable modification, from the methods prevalent in various parts of India. It was introduced by the Portuguese, and continued by the Dutch, the latter of whom had two elephant hunts in each year, and conducted their operations on so large a scale, that the annual export, after supplying the Government establishments, was from one hundred to one hundred and fifty elephants, taken principally in the vicinity of Matura, in the southern province, and marched for shipment to Manaar.[2]

[1] In the *Philosophical Transactions* for 1701, there is "An Account of the taking of Elephants in Ceylon, by Mr. STRACHAN, a Physician who lived seventeen years there," in which the author describes the manner in which they were shipped by the Dutch, at Matura, Galle, and Negombo. A piece of strong sail-cloth having been wrapped round the elephant's chest and stomach he was forced into the sea between two tame ones, and there made fast to a boat. The tame ones then returned to land, and he swam after the boat to the ship, where tackle was reeved to the sail-cloth, and he was hoisted on board.

"But a better way has been invented lately," says Mr. Strachan; "a large flat-bottomed vessel is prepared, covered with planks like a floor; so that this floor is almost of a height with the key. Then the sides of the key and the vessel are adorned with green branches, so that the elephant sees no water till he is in the ship." (*Phil. Trans.* vol. xxiii. No. 227, p. 1051.)

[2] VALENTYN, *Oud en Nieuw Oost-Indien*, ch. xv. p. 272.

The custom in Bengal is to construct a strong enclosure (called a *keddah*), in the heart of the forest, formed of the trunks of trees firmly secured by transverse beams and buttresses, and leaving a gate for the entrance of the elephants. A second enclosure, opening from the first, contains water (if possible a rivulet); this, again, communicates with a third, which terminates in a funnel-shaped passage, too narrow to admit of an elephant turning, and within this the captives being driven in line, are secured with ropes introduced from the outside, and led away in custody of tamed ones trained for the purpose.

The *keddah* being prepared, the first operation is to drive the elephants towards it, for which purpose vast bodies of men fetch a compass in the forest around the haunts of the herds, contracting it by degrees till they complete the enclosure of a certain area, round which they kindle fires, and cut footpaths through the jungle, to enable the watchers to communicate and combine. All this is performed in cautious silence and by slow approaches, to avoid alarming the herd. A fresh circle nearer to the *keddah* is then formed in the same way, and into this the elephants are admitted from the first one, the hunters following from behind, and lighting new fires around the newly inclosed space. Day after day the process is repeated; till the drove having been brought sufficiently close to make the final rush, the whole party close in from all sides, and with drums, guns, shouts, and flambeaux, force the terrified animals to enter the fatal enclosure, when the passage is barred behind them, and retreat rendered impossible.

Their efforts to escape are repressed by the crowd, who drive them back from the stockade with spears and flaming torches; and at last compel them to pass on into the second inclosure. Here they are detained for a short time, and their feverish exhaustion relieved by free access to water;—until at last, being tempted by food, or otherwise induced to trust themselves in the narrow outlet, they are one after another made fast by ropes, passed in through the palisade; and picketed in the adjoining woods to enter on their course of systematic training.

These arrangements vary in different districts of Bengal; and the method adopted in Ceylon differs in many essential particulars from them all; the keddah, or, as it is here called, the corral or *korahl*[1] (from the Portuguese *curral*, a "cattle-pen"), consists of but one enclosure instead of three. A stream or watering-place is not uniformly enclosed within it, because, although water is indispensable after the long thirst and exhaustion of the captives, it has been found that a pond or rivulet within the corral itself adds to the difficulty of leading them out, and increases their reluctance to leave it; besides which, the smaller ones are often smothered by the others in their eagerness to crowd into the water. The funnel-shaped outlet is also dispensed with, as the animals are liable to bruise and injure themselves within the narrow stockade; and should one of them die in it, as is too often the case in the midst of

[1] It is thus spelled by WOLF, in his *Life and Adventures*, p. 144. *Corral* is at the present day a household word in South America, and especially in La Plata, to designate an *enclosure for cattle*.

the struggle, the difficulty of removing so great a carcase is extreme. The noosing and securing them, therefore, takes place in Ceylon within the area of the first enclosure into which they enter, and the dexterity and daring displayed in this portion of the work far surpasses that of merely attaching the rope through the openings of the paling, as in an Indian keddah.

One result of this change in the system is manifested in the increased proportion of healthy elephants eventually secured and trained out of the number originally enclosed. The reason of this is obvious: under the old arrangements, months were consumed in the preparatory steps of surrounding and driving in the herds, which at last arrived so wasted by excitement and exhausted by privation that numbers died within the corral itself, and still more under the process of training. But in later years the labour of months has been reduced to weeks, and the elephants are driven in fresh and full of vigour, so that comparatively few are lost either in the enclosure or the stables. A conception of the whole operation from commencement to end will be best conveyed by describing the progress of an elephant corral as I witnessed it in 1847 in the great forest on the banks of the Alligator River, the Kimbul-oya, in the district of Kornegalle, about thirty miles north-west of Kandy.

Kornegalle, or Kurunai-galle, was one of the ancient capitals of the island, and the residence of its kings from A.D. 1319 to 1347.[1] The dwelling-house of the principal civil officer in charge of the district now

[1] See Sir J. EMERSON TENNENT's *Ceylon*, vol. I. pt. III. ch. xii. p. 415.

occupies the site of the former palace, and the ground is strewn with fragments of columns and carved stones, the remnants of the royal buildings. The modern town consists of the bungalows of the European officials, each surrounded with its own garden; two or three streets inhabited by Dutch descendents and by Moors; and a native bazaar, with the ordinary array of rice and curry stuffs and cooking chattees of brass or burnt clay.

The charm of the village is the unusual beauty of its position. It rests within the shade of an enormous rock of gneiss upwards of 600 feet in height, nearly denuded of verdure, and so rounded and worn by time that it has acquired the form of a couchant elephant, from which it derives its name of Aetagalla, the Rock of the Tusker.[1] But Aetagalla is only the last eminence in a range of similarly-formed rocky mountains, which here terminate abruptly; and which, from the fantastic shapes into which their gigantic outlines have been wrought by the action of the atmosphere, are called by the names of the Tortoise Rock, the Eel Rock, and the Rock of the Tusked Elephant. So impressed are the Singhalese by the aspect of these stupendous masses that in ancient grants lands are conveyed in perpetuity, or "so long as the sun and the moon, so long as Aetagalla and Andagalla shall endure."[2]

[1] Another enormous mass of gneiss is called the Kuruminiagalla, or the Beetle-rock, from its resemblance in shape to the back of that insect, and hence is said to have been derived the name of the town, *Kuruna-galle* or Korne-galle.

[2] FORBES quotes a Tamil conveyance of land, the purchaser of which is to "possess and enjoy it as long as the sun and the moon, the earth and its vegetables, the mountains and the River Cauvery exist." (*Oriental Memoirs*, vol. ii. chap. ii.) It will not fail

Kornegalle is the resort of Buddhists from the remotest parts of the island, who come to visit an ancient temple on the summit of the great rock, to which access is had from the valley below by means of steep paths and steps hewn out of the solid stone. Here the chief object of veneration is a copy of the sacred footstep hollowed in the granite, similar to that which confers sanctity on Adam's Peak, the towering apex of which, about forty miles distant, the pilgrims can discern from Aetagalla.

At times the heat at Kornegalle is intense, in consequence of the perpetual glow diffused from these granite cliffs. The warmth they acquire during the blaze of noon becomes almost intolerable towards evening, and the sultry night is too short to permit the rocks to cool between the setting and the rising of the sun. The district is also liable to occasional droughts when the watercourses fail, and the tanks become dry. One of these calamities occurred about the period of my visit, and such was the suffering of the wild animals that numbers of crocodiles and bears made their way into the town to drink at the wells. The soil is prolific in the extreme; rice, cotton, and dry grain are cultivated largely in the valley. Every cottage is surrounded by gardens of cocoa-nuts, arecas, jak-fruit and coffee; the slopes, under tillage, are covered with luxuriant vegetation, and, as far as the eye can reach on every side,

to be observed, that the same figure was employed in Hebrew literature as a type of duration—"They shall fear thee, *so long as the sun and moon endure;* throughout all generations." (Psalm lxxii. 5, 17.)

there are dense forests intersected by streams, in the shade of which the deer and the elephant abound.

In 1847 arrangements were made for one of the great elephant hunts for the supply of the Civil Engineer's Department, and the spot fixed on by Mr. Morris, the Government officer who conducted the corral, was on the banks of the Kimbul river, about fifteen miles from Kornegalle. The country over which we rode to the scene of the approaching capture showed traces of the recent drought, the fields lay to a great extent untilled, owing to the want of water, and the tanks, almost reduced to dryness, were covered with the leaves of the rose-coloured lotus.

Our cavalcade was as oriental as the scenery through which it moved; the Governor and the officers of his staff and household formed a long cortége, escorted by the native attendants, horse-keepers, and foot-runners. The ladies were borne in palankins, and the younger individuals of the party carried in chairs raised on poles, and covered with cool green awnings made of the fresh leaves of the talipat palm.

After traversing the cultivated lands, the path led across open glades of park-like verdure and beauty, and at last entered the great forest under the shade of ancient trees wreathed to their crowns with climbing plants and festooned by natural garlands of convolvulus and orchids. Here silence reigned, disturbed only by the murmuring hum of glittering insects, or the shrill clamour of the plum-headed parroquet and the flute-like calls of the golden oriole.

We crossed the broad sandy beds of two rivers overarched by tall trees, the most conspicuous of which is the kombook,[1] from the calcined bark of which the natives extract a species of lime to be used with their betel. And from the branches hung suspended over the water the gigantic pods of the huge puswael bean,[2] the sheath of which measures six feet long by five or six inches broad.

On ascending the steep bank of the second stream, we found ourselves in front of the residences which had been extemporised for our party in the immediate vicinity of the corral. These cool and enjoyable structures were formed of branches and thatched with palm leaves and fragrant lemon grass; and in addition to a dining-room and suites of bedrooms fitted with tent furniture, they included kitchens, stables, and storerooms, all run up by the natives in the course of a few days.

In former times, the work connected with these elephant hunts was performed by the "forced labour" of the natives, as part of that feudal service which under the name of "raja-kariya" was extorted from the Singhalese during the rule of their native sovereigns. This system was continued by the Portuguese and Dutch, and prevailed under the British Government till its abolition by the Earl of Ripon in 1832. Under it from fifteen hundred to two thousand men under the orders of their headmen, used to be occupied, in constructing the corral, driving in the elephants, maintaining the cordon of

[1] *Pentaptera paniculata.*

[2] *Entada pursætha.*

watch-fires and watchers, and conducting all the laborious operations of the capture. Since the abolition of raja-kariya, however, no difficulty has been found in obtaining the voluntary co-operation of the natives on these exciting occasions. The Government defrays the expense of that portion of the preparations which involves actual cost, such as the skilled labour expended in the erection of the corral and its appurtenances, and the providing of spears, ropes, arms, flutes, drums, gunpowder, and other necessaries for the occasion.

The period of the year selected is that which least interferes with the cultivation of the rice-lands (in the interval between seed time and harvest), and the people themselves, in addition to the enjoyment of the sport, have a personal interest in reducing the number of elephants, which inflict serious injury on their gardens and growing crops. For a similar reason the priests encourage the practice, because the elephants destroy their sacred Bo-trees, of the leaves of which they are passionately fond; besides which it promotes the facility for obtaining elephants for the processions of the temples: and the Raté-mahat-meyas and headmen have a pride in exhibiting the number of retainers who follow them to the field, and the performances of their tame elephants which they lend for the business of the corral. Thus vast numbers of the peasantry are voluntarily occupied for many weeks in putting up the stockades, cutting paths through the jungle, and relieving the beaters engaged in surrounding and driving in the elephants.

In selecting the scene for an elephant hunt a position is chosen which lies on some old and frequented route of

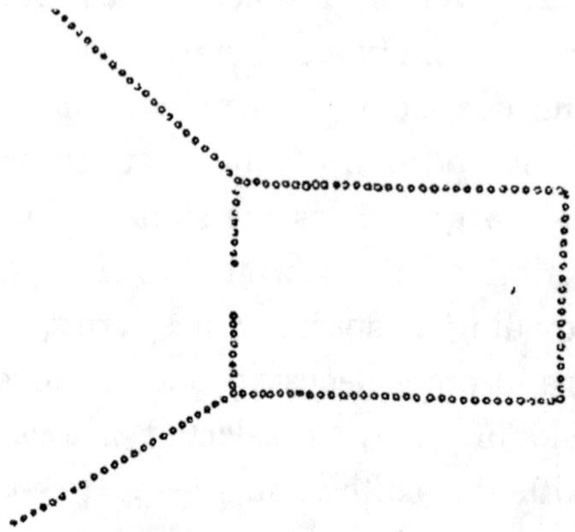

GROUND PLAN OF A CORRAL.

the animals, in their periodical migrations in search of forage and water; and the vicinity of a stream is indis-

METHOD OF FENCING A CORRAL.

pensable, not only for the supply of the elephants during the time spent in inducing them to approach the

enclosure, but to enable them to bathe and cool themselves throughout the process of training after capture.

In constructing the corral itself, care is taken to avoid disturbing the trees or the brushwood within the included space, and especially on the side by which the elephants are to approach, where it is essential to conceal the stockade as much as possible by the density of the foliage. The trees used in the structure are from ten to twelve inches in diameter; and are sunk about three feet in the earth, so as to leave a length of from twelve to fifteen feet above ground; with spaces between each stanchion sufficiently wide to permit a man to glide through. The uprights are made fast by transverse beams, to which they are lashed securely by ratans and flexible climbing plants, or as they are called "jungle ropes," and the whole is steadied by means of forked supports, which grasp the tie beams, and prevent the work from being driven outward by the rush of the wild elephants.

On the occasion I am now attempting to describe, the space thus enclosed was about 500 feet in length by 250 wide. At one end an entrance was left open, fitted with sliding bars, so prepared as to be capable of being instantly shut; and from each angle of the end by which the elephants were to approach, two lines of the same strong fencing were continued, and cautiously concealed by the trees; so that if, instead of entering by the open passage, the herd should swerve to right or left, they would find themselves suddenly stopped and forced to retrace their course to the gate.

The preparations were completed by placing a stage for the Governor's party on a group of the nearest trees looking down into the enclosure, so that a view could be had of the entire proceeding, from the entrance of the herd, to the leading out of the captive elephants.

It is hardly necessary to observe that the structure here described, massive as it is, would be entirely ineffectual to resist the shock, if assaulted by the full force of an enraged elephant; and accidents have sometimes happened by the breaking through of the herd; but reliance is placed not so much on the resistance of the stockade as on the timidity of the captives and their unconsciousness of their own strength, coupled with the daring of their captors and their devices for ensuring submission.

The corral being prepared, the beaters address themselves to drive in the elephants. For this purpose it is often necessary to fetch a circuit of many miles in order to surround a sufficient number, and the caution to be observed involves patience and delay; as it is essential to avoid alarming the animals, which might otherwise escape. Their disposition being essentially peaceful, and their only impulse to browse in solitude and security, they withdraw instinctively before the slightest intrusion, and advantage is taken of this timidity and love of seclusion to cause only just such an amount of disturbance as will induce them to retire slowly in the direction which it is desired they should take. Several herds are by this means concentrated within such an area as will admit of their being completely surrounded by the watchers; and day after day, by slow degrees, they are moved gradually onwards towards the immediate confines of the corral. When their suspicions become awakened and they exhibit restlessness and alarm, bolder measures are adopted for preventing their escape. Fires are kept burning at ten paces apart, night and day, along the circumference of the area within which they are detained; a corps of from two to three thousand beaters is completed, and pathways are carefully cleared through the jungle so as to keep open a communication along the entire circuit. The headmen keep up a constant patrol, to see that their followers are alert at their posts, since neglect at any one spot might permit the escape of the herd, and undo in a moment the vigilance of weeks. By this means any attempt of the elephants to break away is generally checked, and on any point threatened a sufficient force can be promptly assembled to drive them back. At last the elephants are forced onwards so close to the enclosure, that the investing cordon is united at either end with the wings of the corral, the whole forming a circuit of about two miles, within which the herd is detained to await the signal for the final drive.

Two months had been spent in these preliminaries, and the preparations had been thus far completed, on the day when we arrived and took our places on the covered stand erected for us, overlooking the entrance to the corral. Close beneath us a group of tame elephants sent by the temples and the chiefs to assist in securing the wild ones, were picketed in the shade, and lazily fanning themselves with leaves. Three distinct herds, whose united numbers were variously represented at from forty to fifty elephants, were enclosed, and were at that moment concealed in the jungle within a short distance of the stockade. Not a sound was permitted to be made, each person spoke to his neighbour in whispers, and such was the silence observed by the multitude of the watchers at their posts, that occasionally we could hear the rustling of the branches as some of the elephants stripped off a leaf.

Suddenly the signal was made, and the stillness of the forest was broken by the shouts of the guard, the rolling of the drums and tom-toms, and the discharge of muskets; and beginning at the most distant side of the area, the elephants were hurried forward at a rapid pace towards the entrance into the corral.

The watchers along the line kept silence only till the herd had passed them, and then joining the riot in their rear they drove them onward with redoubled shouts and deafening noises. The tumult increased as the terrified rout drew near, swelling now on one side now on the other, as the herd in their panic dashed from point to point in their endeavours to force the line, and the crowd of watchers drove them back with screams, discharges of muskets, and the discordant roar of drums.

At length the breaking of the branches and the crackling of the brushwood announced their close approach, and the leader bursting from the jungle rushed wildly forward to within twenty yards of the entrance, followed by the rest of the herd. Another moment and they would have plunged into the open gate, when suddenly they wheeled round, re-entered the forest, and in spite of the hunters resumed their original position. The chief headman came forward and accounted for the freak by saying that a wild pig,[1] an animal which the elephants are said to dislike, had started out of the cover and run across the leader, who would otherwise have held on direct for the corral; and intimated that as the herd was now in the highest pitch of excitement; and it was at all times much more difficult to effect a successful capture by daylight than by night, when the fires and flambeaux act with double effect, it was the wish of the hunters to defer their final effort till the evening, when the darkness would greatly aid their exertions.

After sunset the scene exhibited was of extraordinary interest; the low fires, which had apparently only smouldered in the sunlight, assumed their ruddy glow amidst the darkness, and threw their tinge over the groups collected round them; while the smoke rose in eddies through the rich foliage of the trees. The crowds of spectators maintained a profound silence, and not a sound was perceptible louder than the hum of an insect. On a sudden the stillness was broken by the distant roll of a drum, followed by a discharge of musketry. This was the signal for the renewal of the assault, and the hunters entered the circle with yells and clamour; dry leaves and sticks were flung upon the watch-fires till they blazed aloft, and formed a line of flame on every side, except in

[1] Fire, the sound of a horn, and the grunting of a boar are the three things which the Greeks, in the middle ages, believed the elephant specially to dislike:

Πῦρ δὲ πτοεῖται καὶ κριὸν κερασφόρον,
Καὶ τῶν μονιῶν τὴν βοὴν τὴν ἀθρόαν.

PHILE, *Expositio de Elephante*, I. 177.

the direction of the corral, which was studiously kept dark; and thither the terrified elephants betook themselves, followed by the shouts and racket of their pursuers.

The elephants came on at a rapid pace, trampling down the brushwood and crushing the dry branches; the leader emerged in front of the corral, paused for an instant, stared wildly round, and then rushed madly through the open gate, followed by the rest of the herd. Instantly, as if by magic, the entire circuit of the corral, which up to this moment had been kept in profound darkness, blazed with thousands of lights, every hunter, on the instant that the elephants entered, rushing forward to the stockade with a torch kindled at the nearest watch-fire.

The elephants first dashed to the very extremity of the enclosure, and being brought up by the fence, retreated to regain the gate, but found it closed. Their terror was sublime: they hurried round the corral at a rapid pace, but saw it now girt by fire on every side; they attempted to force the stockade, but were driven back by the guards with spears and flambeaux; and on whichever side they approached they were repulsed with shouts and volleys of musketry. Collecting into one group, they would pause for a moment in apparent bewilderment, then burst off in another direction, as if it had suddenly occurred to them to try some point which they had before overlooked; but, again baffled, they slowly returned to their forlorn resting-place in the centre of the corral.

The attraction of this strange scene was not confined

to the spectators; it extended to the tame elephants which were stationed outside. At the first approach of the flying herd they evinced the utmost interest. Two in particular which were picketed near the front were intensely excited, and continued tossing their heads, pawing the ground, and starting as the noise drew near. At length, when the grand rush into the corral took place, one of them fairly burst from her fastenings and rushed towards the herd, levelling a tree of considerable size which obstructed her passage.[1]

For upwards of an hour the elephants continued to traverse the corral and assail the palisade with unabated energy, trumpeting and screaming with rage after each disappointment. Again and again they attempted to force the gate, as if aware, by experience, that it ought to afford an exit as it had already served as an entrance, but they shrank back stunned and bewildered. By degrees their efforts became less and less frequent. Single ones rushed excitedly here and there, returning sullenly to their companions after each effort; and at last the whole herd, stupefied and exhausted, formed themselves into a single group, drawn up in a circle with the young in the centre, and stood motionless under the dark shade of the trees in the middle of the corral.

[1] The other elephant, a fine tusker, which belonged to Dehigam Raté-mahat-meya, continued in extreme excitement throughout all the subsequent operations of the capture, and at last, after attempting to break its way into the corral, shaking the bars with its forehead and tusks, it went off in a state of frenzy into the jungle. A few days after the Aratchy went in search of it with a female decoy, and watching its approach, sprang fairly on the infuriated beast, with a pair of sharp hooks in his hands, which he pressed into tender parts in front of the shoulder, and thus held the elephant firmly till chains were passed over its legs, and it permitted itself to be led quietly away.

Preparations were now made to keep watch during the night, the guard was reinforced around the enclosure, and wood heaped on the fires to keep up a high flame till sunrise.

Three herds had been originally entrapped by the beaters outside; but with characteristic instinct they had each kept clear of the other, taking up different stations in the space invested by the watchers. When the final drive took place one herd only had entered the enclosure, the other two keeping behind; and as the gate had to be instantly shut on the first division, the last were unavoidably excluded and remained concealed in the jungle. To prevent their escape, the watchers were ordered to their former stations, the fires were replenished; and all precautions having been taken, we returned to pass the night in our bungalows by the river.

CHAPTER II.

THE CAPTIVES.

As our sleeping-place was not above two hundred yards from the corral, we were awakened frequently during the night by the din of the multitude who were bivouacking in the forest, by the merriment round the watch-fires, and now and then by the shouts with which the guards repulsed some sudden charge of the elephants in attempts to force the stockade. But at daybreak, on going down to the corral, we found all still and vigilant. The fires were allowed to die out as the sun rose, and the watchers who had been relieved were sleeping near the great fence, the enclosure on all sides being surrounded by crowds of men and boys with spears or white peeled wands about ten feet long, whilst the elephants within were huddled together in a compact group, no longer turbulent and restless, but exhausted and calm, and utterly subdued by apprehension and amazement at all that had been passing around them.

Nine only had been as yet entrapped,[1] of which three

[1] In some of the elephant hunts conducted in the southern provinces of Ceylon by the earlier British Governors, as many as 170 and 200 elephants were secured in a single corral, of which a portion only were taken out for the public service, and the rest shot, the motive being to rid the neighbourhood of them, and thus protect the crops from destruction. On the

were very large, and two were little creatures but a few months old. One of the large ones was a "rogue," and being unacknowledged by the rest of the herd, he was not admitted to their circle, although permitted to stand near them.

Meanwhile, preparations were making outside to conduct the tame elephants into the corral, in order to secure the captives. Noosed ropes were in readiness; and far apart from all stood a party of the out-caste Rodiyas, the only tribe who will touch a dead carcase, to whom, therefore, the duty is assigned of preparing the fine flexible rope for noosing, which is made from the fresh hides of the deer and the buffalo.

At length, the bars which secured the entrance to the corral were cautiously withdrawn, and two trained elephants passed stealthily in, each ridden by its mahout (or *ponnekella*, as the keeper is termed in Ceylon), and one attendant; and carrying a strong collar, formed by coils of rope made from coco-nut fibre, from which hung on either side cords of elk's hide, prepared with a ready noose. Along with these, and concealed behind them, the headmen of the "*cooroowe*" or noosers, crept in, eager to secure the honour of taking the first elephant, a distinction which this class jealously contests with the mahouts of the chiefs and temples. He was a wiry little man, nearly seventy years old, who had served in the same capacity under the last Kandyan king, and he wore two silver bangles, which had been conferred

occasion here described, the object being to secure only as many as were required for the Government stud, it was not sought to entrap more than could conveniently be attended to and trained after capture.

on him in testimony of his prowess. He was accompanied by his son, named Ranghani, equally renowned for his courage and dexterity.

On this occasion ten tame elephants were in attendance; two were the property of an adjoining temple (one of which had been caught but the year before, yet it was now ready to assist in capturing others), four belonged to the neighbouring chiefs, and the rest, including the two which first entered the corral, were part of the Government stud. Of the latter, one was of great age, having been in the service of the Dutch and English Governments in succession for upwards of a century.[1] The other, called by her keeper "Siribeddi," was about fifty years old, and distinguished for gentleness and docility. She was a most accomplished decoy, and evinced the utmost relish for the sport. Having entered the corral noiselessly, carrying a mahout on her shoulders with the headman of the noosers seated behind him, she moved slowly along with a sly composure and an assumed air of easy indifference; sauntering leisurely in the direction of the captives, and halting now and then to pluck a bunch of grass or a few leaves as she passed. As she approached the herd, they put themselves in motion to meet her, and the leader, having advanced in front and passed his trunk gently over her head, turned and paced slowly back to his dejected companions. Siribeddi followed with the same listless step, and drew herself up close behind him, thus affording the nooser

[1] This elephant is since dead; she grew infirm and diseased, and died at Colombo in 1848. Her skeleton is now in the Museum of the Natural History Society at Belfast.

an opportunity to stoop under her and slip the noose over the hind foot of the wild one. The latter instantly perceived his danger, shook off the rope, and turned to attack the man. He would have suffered for his temerity had not Siribeddi protected him by raising her trunk and driving the assailant into the midst of the herd, when the old man, being slightly wounded, was helped out of the corral, and his son, Ranghani, took his place.

The herd again collected in a circle, with their heads towards the centre. The largest male was singled out, and two tame ones pushed boldly in, one on either side of him, till the three stood nearly abreast. He made no resistance, but betrayed his uneasiness by shifting restlessly from foot to foot. Ranghani now crept up, and, holding the rope open with both hands (its other extremity being made fast to Siribeddi's collar), and watching the instant when the wild elephant lifted its hind-foot, succeeded in passing the noose over its leg, drew it close, and fled to the rear. The two tame elephants instantly fell back, Siribeddi stretched the rope to its full length, and, whilst she dragged out the captive, her companion placed himself between her and the herd to prevent any interference.

In order to tie him to a tree he had to be drawn backwards some twenty or thirty yards, making furious resistance, bellowing in terror, plunging on all sides, and crushing the smaller timber, which bent like reeds beneath his clumsy struggles. Siribeddi drew him steadily after her, and wound the rope round the proper tree, holding it all the time at its full tension, and stepping

NOOSING WILD ELEPHANTS.

cautiously across it when, in order to give it a second turn, it was necessary to pass between the tree and the elephant. With a coil round the stem, however, it was beyond her strength to haul the prisoner close up, which was, nevertheless, necessary in order to make him perfectly fast; but the second tame one, perceiving the difficulty, returned from the herd, confronted the struggling prisoner, pushed him shoulder to shoulder, and head to head, forcing him backwards, whilst at every step Siribeddi hauled in the slackened rope till she brought him fairly up to the foot of the tree, where he was made fast by the cooroowe people. A second noose was then passed over the other hind-leg, and secured like the first, both legs being afterwards hobbled together by ropes made from the fibre of the kitool or jaggery palm, which, being more flexible than that of the coco nut, occasions less formidable ulcerations. The two decoys then ranged themselves, as before, abreast of the prisoner on either side, thus enabling Ranghani to stoop under them and noose the two fore-feet as he had already done the hind; and these ropes being made fast to a tree in front, the capture was complete, and the tame elephants and keepers withdrew to repeat the operation on another of the herd.

As long as the tame ones stood beside him the poor animal remained comparatively calm and almost passive under his distress, but the moment they moved off, and he was left utterly alone, he made the most surprising efforts to set himself free and rejoin his companions. He felt the ropes with his trunk and tried to untie the numerous knots; he drew backwards to liberate his fore-legs, then leaned forward to extricate the hind ones, till every branch of the tall tree quivered with his struggles. He screamed in anguish, with his proboscis raised high in air, then falling on his side he laid his head to the ground, first his cheek and then his

brow, and pressed down his doubled-in trunk as though he would force it into the earth; then suddenly rising he balanced himself on his forehead and fore-legs, holding his hind-feet fairly off the ground. This scene of distress continued some hours, with occasional pauses of apparent stupor, after which the struggle was from time to time renewed convulsively, and as if by some sudden impulse; but at last the vain strife subsided, and the poor animal remained perfectly motionless, the image of exhaustion and despair.

Meanwhile Ranghani presented himself in front of the Governor's stage to claim the accustomed largesse for tying the first elephant. He was rewarded by a

shower of rupees, and retired to resume his perilous duties in the corral.

The rest of the herd were now in a state of pitiable dejection, and pressed closely together as if under a sense of common misfortune. For the most part they stood at rest in a compact body, fretful and uneasy. At intervals one more impatient than the rest would move out a few steps to reconnoitre; the others would follow at first slowly, then at a quicker pace, and at last the whole herd would rush off furiously to renew the often-baffled attempt to storm the stockade.

There was a strange combination of the sublime and the ridiculous in these abortive onsets; the appearance of prodigious power in their ponderous limbs, coupled with the almost ludicrous shuffle of their clumsy gait, and the fury of their apparently resistless charge, converted in an instant into timid retreat. They rushed madly down the enclosure, their backs arched, their tails extended, their ears spread, and their trunks raised high above their heads, trumpeting and uttering shrill screams, yet when one step further would have dashed the opposing fence into fragments, they stopped short on a few white rods being pointed at them through the paling;[1] and, on catching the derisive shouts of the crowd, they turned in utter discomfiture, and after an objectless circle through the corral, they paced slowly back to their melancholy halting-place in the shade.

The crowd, chiefly comprised of young men and boys, exhibited astonishing nerve and composure at such moments, rushing up to the point towards which the elephants charged, pointing their wands at their trunks, and keeping up the continual cry of *whoop! whoop!* which invariably turned them to flight.

[1] The fact of the elephant exhibiting timidity, on having a long rod pointed towards him, was known to the Romans; and PLINY, quoting from the annals of PISO, relates, that in order to inculcate contempt for want of courage in the elephant, they were introduced into the circus during the triumph of METELLUS, after the conquest of the Carthaginians in Sicily, and *driven round the area by workmen holding blunted spears*,—"Ab operariis hastas præpilatas habentibus, per circum totum actos." (*Nat. Hist.* lib. viii. c. 6.)

The second victim singled out from the herd was secured in the same manner as the first. It was a female. The tame ones forced themselves in on either side as before, cutting her off from her companions, whilst Ranghani stooped under them to attach the fatal noose, and Siribeddi dragged her out amidst unavailing struggles, when she was made fast by each leg to the nearest group of strong trees. When the noose was placed upon her fore-foot, she seized it with her trunk and succeeded in carrying it to her mouth, where she would speedily have severed it had not a tame elephant interfered, and placing his foot on the rope pressed it downwards out of her jaws. The individuals who acted as leaders in the successive charges on the palisades were always those selected by the noosers, and the operation of tying each, from the first approaches of the decoys, till the captive was left alone by the tree, occupied on an average somewhat less than three-quarters of an hour.

It is strange that in these encounters the wild elephants made no attempt to attack or dislodge the mahouts or the cooroowes, who rode on the tame ones. They moved in the very midst of the herd, any individual in which could in a moment have pulled the riders from their seats ; but no attempt was made to molest them.[1]

As one after another their leaders were entrapped and

[1] "In a corral, to be on a tame elephant, seems to insure perfect immunity from the attacks of the wild ones. I once saw the old chief Mollegodde ride in amongst a herd of wild elephants, on a small elephant ; so small that the Adigar's head was on a level with the back of the wild animals : I felt very nervous, but he rode right in among them, and received not the slightest molestation."—*Letter from* Major SKINNER.

forced away from them, the remainder of the group evinced increased emotion and excitement; but whatever may have been their sympathy for their lost com-

panions, their alarm seemed to prevent them at first from following them to the trees to which they had been tied. In passing them afterwards they sometimes stopped, mutually entwined their trunks, lapped them round each other's limbs and neck, and exhibited the most touching distress at their detention, but made no attempt to disturb the cords that bound them.

The variety of disposition in the herd as evidenced by difference of demeanour was very remarkable : some submitted with comparatively little resistance ; whilst others in their fury dashed themselves on the ground with a force sufficient to destroy any weaker animal. They vented their rage upon every tree and plant within reach ; if small enough to be torn down, they levelled them with their trunks, and stripping them of their leaves and branches, tossed them wildly over their heads on all sides. Some in their struggles made no noise, whilst others bellowed and trumpeted furiously, then uttered short convulsive screams, and at last, exhausted and hopeless, gave vent to their anguish in low and piteous moanings. Some, after a few violent efforts of this kind, lay motionless on the ground, with no other indication of suffering than the tears which suffused their eyes and flowed incessantly. Others in all the vigour of their rage exhibited the most surprising contortions ; and to us who had been accustomed to associate with the unwieldy bulk of the elephant the idea that he must of necessity be stiff and inflexible, the attitudes into which they forced themselves were scarcely credible. I saw one lie with the cheek pressed to the earth, and the fore-legs stretched in front, whilst the body was twisted round till the hind legs extended in the opposite direction.

It was astonishing that their trunks were not wounded by the violence with which they flung them on all sides. One twisted his proboscis into such fantastic shapes, that it resembled the writhings of a gigantic worm; he coiled it and uncoiled it with restless rapidity, suddenly unfolding it to its full length, and coiling it up again like a watch-spring. Another, which lay otherwise motionless in all the stupor of hopeless anguish, slowly beat the ground with the extremity of his trunk, as a man in despair beats his knee with the palm of his hand.

They displayed an amount of sensitiveness and delicacy of touch in the foot, which was very remarkable in a limb of such clumsy dimensions and protected by so thick a covering. The noosers could always force them to lift it from the ground by the gentlest touch of a leaf or twig, apparently applied so as to tickle; but the imposition of the rope was instantaneously perceived, and if it could not be reached by the trunk the other foot was applied to feel its position, and if possible remove it before the noose could be drawn tight.

One practice was incessant with almost the entire herd: in the intervals between their struggles they beat the ground with their fore-feet, and taking up the dry earth in a coil of the trunk, they flung it dexterously over every part of their body. Even when lying down the sand within reach was thus collected and scattered over their limbs; then inserting the extremity of the trunk in their mouths, they withdrew a quantity of water, which they discharged over their backs, repeating the operation again and again, till the dust was thoroughly saturated. I was astonished at the quantity of water thus applied, which was sufficient when the elephant, as was generally the case, had worked the spot where he lay into a hollow, to convert its surface into a coating of mud. Seeing that the herd had been now twenty-four hours without access to water of any kind, surrounded by watch-fires, and exhausted by struggling and terror, the supply of moisture an elephant is capable of containing in the receptacle attached to his stomach must be very considerable.

The conduct of the tame ones during all these proceedings was truly wonderful. They displayed the most perfect conception of every movement, both of the object to be attained, and of the means to accomplish it. They manifested the utmost enjoyment in what was going on. There was no ill-humour, no malignity in the spirit displayed, in what was otherwise a heartless proceeding, but they set about it in a way that showed a thorough relish for it, as an agreeable pastime. Their caution was as remarkable as their sagacity; there was no hurrying, no confusion, they never ran foul of the ropes, were never in the way of the animals already noosed; and amidst the most violent struggles, when the tame ones had frequently to step across the captives, they in no instance trampled on them, or occasioned the slightest accident or annoyance. So far from this, they saw intuitively a difficulty or a danger, and addressed themselves unbidden to remove it. In tying up one of the larger elephants, he contrived before he could be hauled close up to the tree, to walk once or twice round it, carrying the rope with him; the decoy, perceiving the advantage he had thus gained over the nooser, walked up of her own accord, and pushed him backwards with her head, till she made him unwind himself again; upon which the rope was hauled tight and made fast. More than once, when a wild one was extending his trunk, and would have intercepted the rope about to be placed over his leg, Siribeddi, by a sudden motion of her own trunk, pushed his aside, and prevented him; and on one occasion, when successive efforts had failed to put the noose over the fore-leg of an elephant which was already secured by one foot, but which wisely put the other to the ground as often as it was attempted to pass the noose under it, I saw the decoy watch her opportunity, and when his foot was again raised, suddenly push in her own leg beneath it, and hold it up till the noose was attached and drawn tight.

One could almost fancy there was a display of dry humour in the manner in which the decoys thus played with the fears of the wild herd, and made light of their

ATTITUDES OF CAPTURED ELEPHANTS.

efforts at resistance. When reluctant they shoved them forward, when violent they drove them back ; when the wild ones threw themselves down, the tame ones butted them with head and shoulders, and forced them up again. And when it was necessary to keep them down, they

knelt upon them, and prevented them from rising, till the ropes were secured.

At every moment of leisure they fanned themselves with a bunch of leaves, and the graceful ease with which an elephant uses his trunk on such occasions is very striking. It is doubtless owing to the combination of a circular with a horizontal movement in that flexible limb ;

but it is impossible to see an elephant fanning himself without being struck by the singular elegance of motion which he displays. The tame ones, too, indulged in the luxury of dusting themselves with sand, by flinging it from their trunks; but it was a curious illustration of their delicate sagacity, that so long as the mahout was on their necks, they confined themselves to flinging the dust along their sides and stomach, as if aware, that to throw it over their heads and back would cause annoyance to their riders.

One of the decoys which rendered good service, and was obviously held in special awe by the wild herd, was a tusker belonging to Dehigame Raté-mahat-meya. It was not that he used his tusks for purposes of offence, but he was enabled to insinuate himself between two elephants by wedging them in where he could not force his head; besides which they assisted him in raising up the fallen and refractory with greater ease. In some instances where the intervention of the other decoys failed to reduce a wild one to order, the mere presence and approach of the tusker seemed to inspire fear, and insure submission, without more active intervention.

I do not know whether it was the surprising qualities exhibited by the tame elephants that cast the courage and dexterity of the men into the shade, but even when supported by the presence, the sagacity, and co-operation of these wonderful creatures, the part sustained by the noosers can bear no comparison with the address and daring displayed by the *picador* and *matador* in a Spanish bull-fight. They certainly possessed great quickness of eye in watching the slightest movement of the elephant, and great expertness in flinging the noose over its foot and attaching it firmly before the animal could tear it off with its trunk; but in all this they had the cover of the decoys to conceal them; and their shelter behind which to retreat. Apart from the services which, from their prodigious strength, the tame elephants alone are capable of rendering, in dragging out and securing the captives, it is perfectly obvious that without their co-operation the utmost prowess and dexterity of the hunters would not avail nor embolden them, unsupported, to enter the corral and ensnare and lead out a single captive.

Of the two tiny elephants which were entrapped, one was about ten months old, the other somewhat more. The smaller one had a little bolt head covered with woolly brown hair, and was the most amusing and interesting miniature imaginable. Both kept constantly with the herd, trotting after them in every charge; when the others stood at rest they ran in and out between the legs of the older ones; and not their own mothers alone, but every female in the group, caressed them in turn.

The dam of the youngest was the second elephant singled out by the noosers, and as she was dragged along by the decoys, the little creature kept by her side till she was drawn close to the fatal tree. The men at first were rather amused than otherwise by its anger; but they found that it would not permit them to place the second noose upon its mother; it ran between her and them, it tried to seize the rope, it pushed them and struck them with its little trunk, till they were forced to drive it back to the herd. It retreated slowly, shouting all the way, and pausing at every step to look back. It then attached itself to the largest female remaining in the group, and placed itself across her fore legs, whilst she hung down her trunk over its side and soothed and caressed it. Here it continued moaning and lamenting, till the noosers had left off securing its mother, when it instantly returned to her side; but as it became troublesome again, attacking every one who passed, it was at last tied up by a rope to an adjoining tree, to which the other young one was also tied. The second little one, equally with its playmate, exhibited great affection for its dam; it went willingly with its captor as far as the tree to which she was fastened, and in passing her stretched out its trunk and tried to rejoin her; but finding itself forced along, it struggled and caught at every twig and branch within its reach, screaming with grief and disappointment.

These two little creatures were the most vociferous of the whole herd, their shouts were incessant, they struggled to attack everyone within reach; and as their bodies were more lithe and pliant than those of greater growth, their contortions were quite wonderful. The most amusing thing was, that in the midst of all their agony and affliction, the little fellows seized on every article of food that was thrown to them, and munched and roared simultaneously.

Amongst the last of the elephants noosed was the *rogue.* Though far more savage than the others, he joined in none of their charges and assaults on the fences, as they uniformly drove him off and would not permit him to enter their circle. When dragged past another of his companions in misfortune, who was lying exhausted on the ground, he flew upon him and attempted to fasten his teeth in his head; this was the only instance of viciousness which occurred during the progress of the corral. When tied up and overpowered, he was at first noisy and violent, but soon lay down peacefully, a sign, according to the hunters, that his death was at hand. Their prognostication proved to be correct; he continued for about twelve hours to cover himself with dust like the others, and to moisten it with water from his trunk; but at length he sunk exhausted, and died so calmly, that having been moving but a few moments before, his death was only perceived by the myriads of black flies by which his body was almost instantly covered, although not one was visible a moment before.[1] The Rodiyas were called

[1] The surprising faculty of vultures for discovering carrion, has been a subject of much speculation, as to whether it be dependent on their power of sight or of scent. It is not, however, more mysterious than the unerring certainty and rapidity with which some of the minor animals, and more especially insects, in warm climates congregate around the offal on which they feed. Circumstanced as they are, they must be guided towards their object mainly if not exclusively by the sense of smell; but that which excites astonishment is the small degree of odour which seems to suffice for the purpose; the subtlety and rapidity with which it traverses and impregnates the air; and the keen and quick perception with which it is taken up by the organs of those creatures. The instance of the scavenger beetles has been already alluded to; the promptitude with which they discern the existence of matter suited to their purposes, and the speed with which they hurry to it from all directions; often from distances as extraordinary, proportionably, as those traversed by the eye of the vulture. In the instance of the dying elephant referred to above, life was barely extinct when the flies, of which not one was visible but a moment before, arrived in clouds and blackened the body by their multitude; scarcely an instant was allowed to elapse for the commencement of decomposition; no odour of putrefaction could be discerned by us who stood close by; yet some peculiar smell of mortality, simultaneously with parting breath, must have summoned them to the feast. Ants exhibit an instinct equally surprising. I have sometimes covered up a particle of refined sugar with paper on the centre of a polished table; and counted the number of minutes which would

in to loose from the tree the ropes that bound him, and two tame elephants being harnessed to the dead body, it was dragged to a distance without the corral.

When every wild elephant had been noosed and tied up, the scene presented was truly oriental. From one to two thousand natives, many of them in gaudy dresses and armed with spears, crowded about the enclosures. Their families too had collected from great distances to see the spectacle; women, whose children clung like little bronzed Cupids by their sides; and girls, many of them in the graceful costume of that part of the country, —a scarf, which, after having been brought round the waist, is thrown over the left shoulder, leaving the right arm and side free and uncovered.

At the foot of each tree was its captive elephant;

elapse before it was fastened on by the small black ants of Ceylon, and a line formed to lower it safely to the floor. Here was a substance which, to our apprehension at least, is altogether inodorous, and yet the quick sense of smell must have been the only conductor of the ants. It has been observed of those fishes which travel overland on the evaporation of the ponds in which they live, that they invariably march in the direction of the nearest water, and even when captured, and placed on the floor of a room, their efforts to escape are always made towards the same point. Is the sense of smell sufficient to account for this display of instinct in them? or is it aided by special organs in the case of the others? Dr. McGee, formerly of the Royal Navy, writing to me on the subject of the instant appearance of flies in the vicinity of dead bodies, says: "In warm climates they do not wait for death to invite them to the banquet. In Jamaica I have again and again seen them settle on a patient, and hardly to be driven away by the nurse, the patient himself saying, 'Here are these flies coming to eat me ere I am dead.' At times they have enabled the doctor, when otherwise he would have been in doubt as to his prognosis, to determine whether the strange apyretic interval occasionally present in the last stage of yellow fever was the fatal lull or the lull of recovery; and 'What say the flies?' has been the settling question. Among many, many cases during a long period I have seen but one recovery after the assembling of the flies. I consider the foregoing as a confirmation of smell being the guide even to the attendants, a cadaverous smell has been perceived to arise from the body of a patient twenty-four hours before death."

some still struggling and writhing in feverish excitement, whilst others, in exhaustion and despair, lay calm and motionless, except that, from time to time, they heaped fresh dust upon their heads. The mellow notes of a Kandyan flute, which was played at a distance, had a striking effect upon one or more of them; they turned their heads in the direction from which the music came, expanded their broad ears, and were evidently soothed with the plaintive sound. The two little ones alone still roared for freedom; they stamped their feet, and blew clouds of dust over their shoulders, brandishing their little trunks aloft, and threatened every one who came within their reach.

At first the older ones, when secured, spurned every offer of food, trampled it under foot, and turned haughtily away. A few, however, as they became more composed, could not resist the temptation of the juicy stems of the plantain, but rolling them under foot, till they detached the layers, they raised them in their trunks, and commenced to chew them listlessly.

On the whole, whilst the sagacity, the composure, and docility of the decoys were such as to excite lively astonishment, it was not possible to withhold high admiration from the calm and dignified demeanour of the captives. Their entire bearing was at variance with the representation made by some of the "sportsmen" who harass them, that they are treacherous, savage, and revengeful; when tormented by the guns of their persecutors, they no doubt display their powers and sagacity in efforts to retaliate or escape; but here their every movement was indicative of innocence and timidity. After a struggle, in which they evinced no disposition to violence or revenge, they submitted with the calmness of despair. Their attitudes were pitiable, their grief was most touching, and their low moaning went to the heart. We could not have borne to witness their distress had their capture been effected by the needless infliction of pain, or had they been destined to ill-treatment afterwards.

It was now about two hours after noon, and the first elephants that had entered the corral having been disposed of, preparations were made to reopen the gate, and drive in the other two herds, over which the watchers were still keeping guard. The area of the inclosure was cleared; and silence was again imposed on the crowds who surrounded the corral. The bars that secured the entrance were withdrawn, and every precaution repeated as before; but as the space inside was now somewhat trodden down, especially near the entrance, by the frequent charges of the last herd, and as it was to be apprehended that the others might be earlier alarmed and retrace their steps, before the barricades could be replaced, two tame ones were stationed inside to protect the men to whom that duty was assigned.

All preliminaries being at length completed, the signal was given; the beaters on the side most distant from the corral closed in with tom-toms and discordant noises; a hedge-fire of musketry was kept up in the rear of the terrified elephants; thousands of voices urged them forward; we heard the jungle crashing as they came on, and at last they advanced through an opening amongst the trees, bearing down all before them like a charge of locomotives. They were led by a huge female, nearly nine feet high, after whom one half of the herd dashed precipitately through the narrow entrance, but the rest, turning suddenly towards the left, succeeded in forcing the cordon of guards and making good their escape to the forest.

No sooner had the others passed in through the gate, than the tame elephants stepped forward from either side, and before the herd could return from the further end of the enclosure, the bars were replaced, the entrance closed, and the men in charge glided outside the stockade. The elephants which had previously been made prisoners within exhibited intense excitement as the fresh din arose around them; they started to their feet, and stretched their trunks in the direction whence they winded the scent of the herd in its headlong flight; and as the latter rushed past, they renewed their struggles to get free and follow. It is not possible to imagine anything more exciting than the spectacle which the wild ones presented careering round the corral, uttering piercing screams, with heads erect and trunks aloft, the very emblems of rage and perplexity, of power and helplessness.

Along with those which entered at the second drive was one that evidently belonged to another herd, and had been separated from it in the *mêlée* when the latter effected their escape, and, as usual, his new companions in misfortune drove him off indignantly as often as he attempted to approach them.

The demeanour of those taken in the second drive differed materially from that of the preceding captives, who, having entered the corral in darkness, suddenly found themselves girt with fire and smoke, and beset by hideous sounds and sights on every side, and were speedily reduced by fear to stupour and submission—whereas, the second herd having passed into the enclosure by daylight, and its area being trodden down in many places, could clearly discern the fences, and were consequently alarmed and enraged at their confinement. They were thus as restless as the others had been calm, and so much more vigorous in their assaults that, on one occasion, their courageous leader, undaunted by the multitude of white wands thrust towards her, was only driven back from the stockade by a hunter hurling a blazing flambeau at her head. Her attitude as she stood repulsed, but still irresolute, was a study for a painter. Her eye dilated, her ears expanded, her back arched like a tiger, and her fore-foot in air, whilst she uttered those hideous screams that are imperfectly described by the term "*trumpeting*."

Although repeatedly passing by the unfortunates from the former drove, the new herd seemed to take no friendly notice of them; they halted inquiringly for a minute, and then resumed their career round the corral, and once or twice in their headlong flight they rushed madly over the bodies of the prostrate captives as they lay in their misery on the ground.

It was evening before the new captives had grown wearied with their furious and repeated charges, and stood still in the centre of the corral collected into a terrified and motionless group. The fires were then re-lighted, the guards redoubled by the addition of the beaters, who were now relieved from the duty of watching in the forest, and the spectators retired to their bungalows for the night.

The business of the *third day* began by noosing and tying up the new captives, and the first sought out was their magnificent leader. Siribeddi and the tame tusker having forced themselves on either side of her, a boy in the service of the rata-mahat-meya succeeded in attaching a rope to her hind-foot. Siribeddi moved off, but feeling her strength insufficient to drag the reluctant prize, she went down on her fore-knees, so as to add the full weight of her body to the pull. The tusker, seeing her difficulty, placed himself in front of the prisoner, and forced her backwards, step by step, till his companion brought her fairly up to the tree, and wound the rope round the stem. Though overpowered by fear, she showed the fullest sense of the nature of the danger she had to apprehend. She kept her head turned towards the noosers, and tried to step in advance of the decoys; in spite of all their efforts, she tore off the first noose from her fore-leg, and placing it under her foot, snapped it into fathom lengths. When finally secured, her writhings were extraordinary. She doubled in her head under her chest, till she lay as round as a hedgehog, and rising again, stood on her fore-feet, and lifting her hind-feet off the ground, she wrung them from side to side, till the great tree above her trembled in every branch.

Before proceeding to catch the remainder we requested that the smaller trees and jungle, which partially obstructed our view, might be broken away, being no longer essential to screen the entrance to the corral; and five of the tame elephants were brought up for the purpose. They felt the strength of each tree with their trunks, then swaying it backwards and forwards, by pushing it with their foreheads, they watched the opportunity when it was in full swing to raise their fore-feet against the stem, and bear it down to the ground.[1] Then tearing off the festoons of climbing plants, and trampling down the smaller branches and brushwood, they pitched them with their tusks, piling them into heaps along the side of the fence.

Amongst the last that was secured was the solitary individual belonging to the fugitive herd. When the tame one attempted to drag him backwards from the tree near which he was noosed, he laid hold of it with his trunk and lay down on his side immoveable. The temple tusker and another were ordered up to assist, and it required the combined efforts of the three elephants to force him along. When dragged to the place at which he was to be tied up, he continued the contest with desperation, and to prevent the second noose being placed on his foot, he sat down on his haunches, almost in the attitude of the "Florentine Boar," keeping his hind-feet beneath him, and defending his fore-feet with his trunk, with which he flung back the rope as often as it was attempted to attach it.

[1] This is precisely the action ascribed by ARISTOTLE to the elephant, when levelling palm trees. *De Anim. Hist.* l. ix. c. 2.

When overpowered and made fast, his grief was most affecting; his violence sunk to utter prostration, and he lay on the ground, uttering choking cries, with tears trickling down his cheeks.

The last operation of the corral was that of slackening the ropes, and marching each captive elephant down to the river between two tame ones. This was effected

very simply. A decoy, with a strong collar round its neck, stood on either side of the wild one, on which a similar collar was formed by successive coils of coco-nut rope; and then, connecting the three collars together, the prisoner was effectually made safe between his two guards. During this operation, it was curious to see how the tame elephant, from time to time, used its trunk to shield the arm of its rider, and ward off the trunk of the prisoner, who resisted the placing the rope round his neck. This done, the nooses were removed from his feet, and he was marched off to the river, in which he and his companions were allowed to bathe; a privilege of which all availed themselves eagerly. Each was then made fast to a tree in the forest, and keepers being assigned to him, with a retinue of leaf-cutters, he was plentifully supplied with his favourite food, and left to the care and tuition of his new masters.

Returning from a spectacle such as I have attempted to describe, one cannot help feeling how immeasurably it exceeds in interest those royal battues where timid deer are driven in crowds to unresisting slaughter; or those vaunted "wild sports" the amusement of which appears to be in proportion to the effusion of blood. Here the only display of power was the imposition of restraint; and though considerable mortality often occurs amongst the animals caught, the infliction of pain, so far from being an incident of the operation, is cautiously avoided, from its tendency to enrage, the policy of the captor being to conciliate and soothe. The whole scene exhibits the most marvellous example of the voluntary alliance of animal sagacity and instinct in active co-operation with human intelligence and courage; and nothing else in nature, not even the chase of the whale, can afford so vivid an illustration of the sovereignty of man over brute creation even when confronted with force in its most stupendous embodiment.

Of the two young elephants which were taken in the

corral, the smallest was sent down to my house at Colombo, where he became a general favourite with the whole family. He attached himself especially to the coachman, who had a little shed erected for him near his own quarters at the stables. But his favourite resort was the kitchen, where he received a daily allowance of milk and plantains, and picked up other delicacies besides. He was innocent and playful in the extreme, and when walking in the grounds he would trot up to me, twine his little trunk round my arm, and coax me to take him to the fruit-trees. In the evening the grass cutters now and then indulged him by permitting him to carry home a load of fodder for the horses, on which occasions he assumed an air of gravity that was highly amusing, showing that he was deeply impressed with the importance and responsibility of the service entrusted to him. Being sometimes permitted to enter the dining-room, and helped to fruit at dessert, he at last learned his way to the sideboard; and on more than one occasion, having stolen in during the absence of the servants, he made a clear sweep of the wine-glasses and china in his endeavours to reach a basket of oranges. For these and similar pranks we were at last forced to put him away. He was sent to the Government stud, at Colombo, where he was affectionately received and adopted by Siribeddi, and he now takes his turn of public duty in the department of the Commissioner of Roads.

CHAPTER III.

CONDUCT IN CAPTIVITY.

THE idea prevailed in ancient times, and obtains even at the present day, that the Indian elephant surpasses that of Africa in sagacity and tractability, and consequently in capacity for training, so as to render its services more available to man. There does not appear to me to be sufficient ground for this conclusion. It originated, in all probability, in the first impressions created by the accounts of the elephant brought back by the Greeks after the Indian expedition of Alexander, and above all by the descriptions of Aristotle, whose knowledge of the animal was derived exclusively from the East. The belief was perpetuated by later writers, especially DIODORUS SICULUS, who says the elephants of India excelled those of Africa in mental capacity not less than in magnitude and strength :—*Oἶ ταῖς τε ἀλκαῖς καὶ ταῖς τοῦ σώματος ῥωμαῖς πολὺ προέχουσι τῶν ἐν τῇ Λιβύῃ γινομένων.* (DIOD. SIC. ii. c. 16.) A long interval elapsed before the elephant of Africa, and its capabilities, became known in Europe. The first elephants brought to Greece by Antipater, were from India, as were also those introduced by Pyrrhus into Italy. Taught by this example, the Carthaginians undertook to employ African elephants in war. Jugurtha led them against Metellus, and Juba against Cæsar; but from inexperienced and deficient training, they proved less effective than the elephants of India,[1] and the historians of these times ascribed to inferiority of race that which was but the result of insufficient education.

It must, however, be remembered that the elephants which, at a later period, astonished the Romans by their sagacity, and whose performances in the amphitheatre have been described by Ælian and Pliny, were brought from Africa, and acquired their accomplishments from European instructors;[2] a sufficient proof that under equally favourable auspices the African species are capable of developing similar docility and powers with those of India. It is one of the facts from which the inferiority of the Negro race has been inferred, that they alone, of all the nations amongst whom the elephant is found, have never manifested ability to domesticate it; and even as regards the more highly developed

[1] ARMANDI, *Hist. Milit. des Eléphants*, liv. i. ch. i. p. 2. It is an interesting fact, noticed by ARMANDI,

that the elephants figured on the coins of Alexander and the Seleucidæ invariably exhibit the characteristics of the Indian type, whilst those on Roman medals can at once be pronounced African, from the peculiarities of the convex forehead and expansive ears. —*Ibid.* liv. i. cap. i. p. 3.

ARMANDI has, with infinite industry, collected from original sources a mass of curious information relative to the employment of elephants in ancient warfare, which he has published under the title of *Histoire Militaire des Eléphants depuis les temps les plus reculés jusqu'à l'introduction des armes à feu.* Paris, 1843.

[2] ÆLIAN, lib. ii. cap. ii.

races who inhabited the valley of the Nile, it is observable that the elephant is nowhere to be found amongst the animals figured on the monuments of ancient Egypt, whilst the camelopard, the lion, and even the hippopotamus are represented. And although in later times the knowledge of the art of training appears to have existed under the Ptolemies, and on the southern shores of the Mediterranean, it admits of no doubt that it was communicated by the more accomplished natives of India who had settled there.[1]

Another favourite doctrine of the earlier visitors to the East seems to me to be equally fallacious; PYRARD, BERNIER, PHILLIPE, THEVENOT, and other travellers in the sixteenth and seventeenth centuries, proclaimed the superiority of the elephant of Ceylon, in size, strength, and sagacity, above those of all other parts of India;[2]

[1] See SCHLEGEL's Essay on the Elephant and the Sphynx, *Classical Journal*, No. lx. Although the trained elephant nowhere appears upon the monuments of the Egyptians, the animal was not unknown to them, and ivory and elephants are figured on the walls of Thebes and Karnac amongst the spoils of Thothmes III. and the tribute paid to Rameses I. The Island of Elephantine, in the Nile, near Assouan (Syene) is styled in hieroglyphical writing "The Land of the Elephant;" but as it is a mere rock, it probably owes its designation to its form. See Sir GARDNER WILKINSON'S *Ancient Egyptians*, vol. i. pl. iv.; vol. v. p. 176. Above the first cataract of the Nile are two small islands, each bearing the name of Phylæ;—quære, is the derivation of this word at all connected with the Arabic term *fil?* See *ante*, p. 4, note. The elephant figured in the sculptures of Nineveh is universally as wild, not domesticated.

[2] This is merely a reiteration of the statement of ÆLIAN, who ascribes to the elephants of Taprobane a vast superiority in size, strength, and intelligence, above those of continental India: Καὶ οἱ δέ γε νησιῶται ἐλέφαντες τῶν ἠπειρωτῶν ἀλκιμώτεροί τε τὴν ῥώμην καὶ μείζους ἰδεῖν εἰσὶ, καὶ θυμοσοφώτεροι δὲ πάντα πάντῃ κρίνοιντο ἄν. —ÆLIAN, *De Nat. Anim.* lib. xvi. cap. xviii.

ÆLIAN also, in the same chapter, states the fact of the shipment of elephants in large boats from Ceylon to the opposite continent of India, for sale to the king of Kalinga; so that the export from Manaar, described in a former passage, has been going on apparently without interruption since the time of the Romans.

and TAVERNIER in particular is supposed to have stated that if a Ceylon elephant be introduced amongst those bred in any other place, by an instinct of nature they do him homage by laying their trunks to the ground, and raising them reverentially. This passage has been so repeatedly quoted in works on Ceylon that it has passed into an aphorism, and is always adduced as a testimony to the surpassing intelligence of the elephants of that island; although a reference to the original shows that Tavernier's observations are not only fanciful in themselves, but are restricted to the supposed excellence of the Ceylon animal *in war.*[1] This estimate of the superiority of the elephant of Ceylon, if it ever prevailed in India, was not current there at a very early period; for in the *Ramayana*, which is probably the oldest epic in the world, the stud of Dasartha, the king of Ayodhya, was supplied with elephants from the Himalaya and the Vindhya Mountains.[2] I have had no opportunity of testing by personal observation the justice of the assumption; but from all that I have heard of the ele-

[1] The expression of TAVERNIER is to the effect, that as compared with all others, the elephants of Ceylon are "plus courageux *à la guerre.*" The rest of the passage is a curiosity:—

"Il faut remarquer ici une chose qu'on aura peut-être de la peine à croire mais qui est toutefois très-véritable: c'est que lorsque quelque roi ou quelque seigneur a quelqu'un de ces éléphants de Ceylan, et qu'on en amène quelque autre des lieux où les marchands vont les prendre, comme d'Achen, de Siam, d'Arakan, de Pégu, du royaume de Boutan, d'Assam, des terres de Cochin et de la côte du Mélinde, dès que les éléphants en voient un de Ceylan, par un instinct de nature, ils lui font la révérence, portant le bout de leur trompe à la terre et la relevant. Il est vrai que les éléphants que les grands seigneurs entretiennent, quand on les amène devant eux, pour voir s'ils sont en bon point, font trois fois une espèce de révérence avec leur trompe, *ce que j'ai vu souvent;* mais ils sont stylés à cela, et leurs maîtres le leur enseignent de bonne heure."—*Les Six Voyages de* J. B. TAVERNIER, lib. iii. ch. 20.

[2] *Ramayana*, sec. vi.; CAREY and MARSHMAN, i. 105; FAUCHE, i. t. p. 66.

phants of the continent, and seen of those of Ceylon, I have reason to conclude that the difference, if not imaginary, is exceptional, and must have arisen in particular and individual instances, from more judicious or elaborate instruction.

The earliest knowledge of the elephant in Europe and the West, was derived from the conspicuous position assigned to it in the wars of the East: in India, from the remotest antiquity, it formed one of the most picturesque, if not the most effective, features in the armies of the native princes.[1] It is more than probable that the

[1] The only mention of the elephant in Sacred History is in the account given in *Maccabees* of the invasion of Egypt by Antiochus, who entered it 170 B.C., "with chariots and elephants, and horsemen, and a great navy." (1 Macc. i. 17.) Frequent allusions to the use of elephants in war occur in both books: and in chap. vi. 34, it is stated that "to provoke the elephants to fight they show them the blood of grapes and of mulberries." The term showed, ἔδειξαν, might be thought to imply that the animals were enraged by the sight of the wine and its colour, but in the Third Book of Maccabees, in the Greek Septuagint, various other passages show that wine, on such occasions, was administered to the elephants to render them furious. (Macc. v. 2, 10, 45.) PHILE mentions the same fact, *De Elephante*, i. 145.

There is a very curious account of the mode in which the Arab conquerors of Scinde, in the 9th and 10th centuries, equipped the elephant for war; which being written with all the particularity of an eye-witness, bears the impress of truth and accuracy. MASSOUDI, who was born in Bagdad at the close of the 9th century, travelled in India in the year A. D. 913, and visited the Gulf of Cambay, the coast of Malabar, and the island of Ceylon:—from a larger account of his journeys he compiled a summary under the title of "*Moroudj al-dzeheb*," or the "*Golden Meadows*," the MS. of which is now in the Bibliothèque Nationale. M. REINAUD, in describing this manuscript, says, on its authority, "The Prince of Mensura, whose dominions lay south of the Indus, maintained eighty elephants trained for war, each of which bore in his trunk a bent cymeter (carthel), with which he was taught to cut and thrust at all confronting him. The trunk itself was effectually protected by a coat of mail, and the rest of the body enveloped in a covering composed jointly of iron and horn. Other elephants were employed in drawing chariots, carrying baggage, and grinding forage, and the performance of all bespoke the utmost intelligence and docility."—REINAUD, *Mémoire sur l'Inde, antérieurement au milieu du* XIe *siècle, d'après les écrivains arabes, persans et chinois.* Paris, M.D.CCC.XLIX. p. 215. See SPRENGER'S English translation of Massoudi, vol. i. p. 383.

earliest attempts to take and train the elephant, were with a view to military uses, and that the art was perpetuated in later times to gratify the pride of the eastern kings, and sustain the pomp of their processions.

An impression prevails even to the present day, that the process of training is tedious and difficult, and the reduction of a full-grown elephant to obedience, slow and troublesome in the extreme.[1] In both particulars, however, the contrary is the truth. The training as it prevails in Ceylon is simple, and the conformity and obedience of the animal are developed with singular rapidity. For the first three days, or till they will eat freely, which they seldom do in a less time, the newly-captured elephants are allowed to remain perfectly quiet; and, if practicable, a tame elephant is tied near them to give the wild ones confidence. Where many elephants are being trained at once, it is customary to put each new captive between the stalls of half-tamed ones, when it soon takes to its food. This stage being attained, training commences by placing tame elephants on either side. The "cooroowe vidahn," or the head of the stables, stands in front of the wild elephants holding a long stick with a sharp iron point. Two men are then stationed one on either side, assisted by the tame elephants, and each holding a *hendoo* or crook[2] towards the wild one's trunk, whilst one or two others rub their hands over his back, keeping up all the while a soothing and plaintive chaunt, interlarded with endearing epithets, such as "ho!

[1] BRODERIP, *Zoological Recreations*, p. 226.

[2] The iron goad with which the keeper directs the movements of the

my son," or "ho! my father," or "my mother," as may be applicable to the age and sex of the captive. The elephant is at first furious, and strikes in all directions with his trunk; but the men in front receiving all these blows on the points of their weapons, the extremity of the trunk becomes so sore that the animal curls it up close, and seldom afterwards attempts to use it offensively. The first dread of man's power being thus established, the process of taking him to bathe between two tame elephants is greatly facilitated, and by lengthening the neck rope, and drawing the feet together as close as possible, the process of laying him down in the water is finally accomplished by the keepers pressing the sharp point of their hendoos over the backbone.

For many days the roaring and resistance which attend the operation are considerable, and it often requires the sagacious interference of the tame elephants to control the refractory wild ones. It soon, however, becomes practicable to leave the latter alone, only

elephants, called a *hendoo* in Ceylon

Medal of Numidia.

and *hawkus* in Bengal, appears to have retained the present shape from the remotest antiquity. It is figured in the medals of Caracalla in the identical

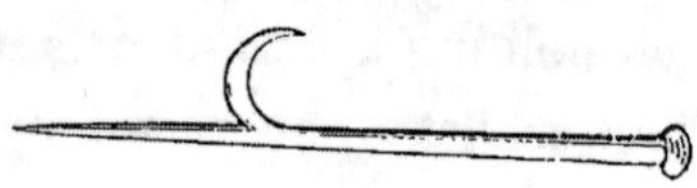

Modern Hendoo.

form in which it is in use at the present day in India.

The Greeks called it ἅρπη, and the Romans *cuspis*.

taking them to and from the stall by the aid of a decoy. This step lasts, under ordinary treatment, for about three weeks, when an elephant may be taken alone with his legs hobbled, and a man walking backwards in front with the point of the hendoo always presented to the elephant's head, and a keeper with an iron crook at each ear. On getting into the water, the fear of being pricked on his tender back induces him to lie down directly on the crook being only held over him *in terrorem.* Once this point has been achieved, the further process of taming is dependent upon the disposition of the creature.[1]

The greatest care is requisite, and daily medicines are applied to heal the fearful wounds on the legs which even the softest ropes occasion. This is the great difficulty of training; for the wounds fester grievously, and months and sometimes years will elapse before an elephant will allow his feet to be touched without indications of alarm and anger.

The observation has been frequently made that the elephants most vicious and troublesome to tame, and

[1] JORDANUS DE SEVERAC, in his *Mirabilia Descripta*, written about the year 1330, thus describes the mode then in use for taming captured elephants in Cambodia:—"And so the wild elephant remaineth caught between the two gates. Then cometh a man *clothed in black or red, with his face covered*, who cruelly thrashes him from above, and crieth out cruelly against him as against a 'thief!' and this goeth on for five or six days; without his getting anything to eat or drink. Then cometh another man with *his face bare and clad in another colour*, who feigneth to smite the first man, and to drive and thrust him away. Then he cometh to the elephant and talketh to him, and with a long spear he scratcheth him, and he kisses him and gives him food. And this goes on for ten or fifteen days, and so by degrees he ventureth down beside him and bindeth him to another elephant. And then after about twenty days he may be taken out to be taught and broken in." (Chap. v.)

the most worthless when tamed, are those distinguished by a thin trunk and flabby pendulous ears. The period of tuition does not appear to be influenced by the size or strength of the animals: some of the smallest give the greatest amount of trouble; whereas, in the instance of the two largest that have been taken in Ceylon within the last thirty years, both were docile in a remarkable degree. One in particular, which was caught and trained by Mr. Cripps, when Government agent, in the Seven Korles, fed from the hand the first night it was secured, and in a very few days evinced pleasure on being patted on the head.[1] There is none so obstinate, not even a *rogue*, that may not, when kindly and patiently treated, be eventually conciliated and reconciled.

The males are generally more unmanageable than the females, and in both an inclination to lie down to rest is regarded as a favourable symptom of approaching tractability, some of the most resolute having been known to stand for months together, even during sleep. Those which are the most obstinate and violent at first are the soonest and most effectually subdued, and generally prove permanently docile and submissive. But those which are sullen or morose, although they may not

[1] This was the largest elephant that had been tamed in Ceylon; he measured upwards of nine feet at the shoulders, and belonged to the caste so highly prized for the temples. He was gentle after his first capture, but his removal from the corral to the stables, though only a distance of six miles, was a matter of the extremest difficulty: his extraordinary strength rendering him more than a match for the attendant decoys. He on one occasion escaped, but was recaptured in the forest; and he afterwards became so docile as to perform a variety of tricks. He was at length ordered to be removed to Colombo; but such was his terror on approaching the fort, that on coaxing him to enter the gate, he became paralysed in the extraordinary way elsewhere alluded to, and died on the spot.

provoke chastisement by their viciousness, are always slower in being trained, and are rarely to be trusted in after-life.[1]

But whatever may be its natural gentleness and docility, the temper of an elephant is seldom to be implicitly relied on in a state of captivity and coercion. The most amenable are subject to occasional fits of stubbornness; and even after years of submission, irritability and resentment will sometimes unaccountably manifest themselves. It may be that the restraints and severer discipline of training have not been entirely forgotten; or that incidents which in ordinary health would be productive of no demonstration whatever, may lead, in moments of temporary illness, to fretfulness and anger.

[1] The natives of Ceylon profess that the high-caste elephants, such as are allotted to the temples, are of all others the most difficult to tame, and M. BLES, the Dutch correspondent of BUFFON, mentions a caste of elephants which he had heard of, as being peculiar to the Kandyan kingdom, that were not higher than a heifer (génisse), covered with hair, and insusceptible of being tamed. (BUFFON, *Supp.* vol. vi. p. 29.) Bishop HEBER, in the account of his journey from Bareilly towards the Himalayas, describes the Raja Gourman Sing, "mounted on a little female elephant, hardly bigger than a Durham ox, and almost as shaggy as a poodle." (*Journ.* ch. xvii.) It will be remembered that the mammoth discovered in 1803 embedded in icy soil in Siberia, was covered with a coat of long hair, with a sort of wool at the roots. Hence there arose the question whether that northern region had been formerly inhabited by a race of elephants, so fortified by nature against cold; or whether the individual discovered had been borne thither by currents from some more temperate latitudes. To the latter theory the presence of hair seemed a fatal objection; but so far as my own observation goes, I believe the elephants are more or less provided with hair. In some it is more developed than in others, and it is particularly observable in the young, which when captured are frequently covered with a woolly fleece, especially about the head and shoulders. In the older individuals in Ceylon, this is less apparent; and in captivity the hair appears to be altogether removed by the custom of the mahouts to rub their skin daily with oil and a rough lump of burned clay. See a paper on the subject, *Asiat. Journ.* N. S. vol. xiv. p. 182, by Mr. G. FAIRHOLME. Fossil remains of elephants of extremely small dimensions have, it is said, been discovered in the island of Malta.

The knowledge of this infirmity led to the popular belief recorded by PHILE, that the elephant had *two hearts*, under the respective influences of which it evinced ferocity or gentleness; subdued by the one to habitual tractability and obedience, but occasionally roused by the other to displays of rage and resistance.[1]

In the process of training, the presence of the tame ones can generally be dispensed with after two months, and the captive may then be ridden by the driver alone; and after three or four months he may, so far as regards docility, be entrusted with labour; but it is undesirable, and even involves the risk of its life, to work an elephant too soon; it has frequently happened that a valuable animal has laid down and died the first time it was tried in harness, from what the natives believe to be "broken heart,"—certainly without any cause inferable from injury or previous disease.[2] It is observable, that till a captured elephant begins to relish food, and grow fat upon it, he becomes so fretted by work, that it kills him in an incredibly short space of time.

[1] Διπλῆς δέ φασιν εὐπορῆσαι καρδίας·
Καὶ τῇ μὲν εἶναι θυμικὸν τὸ θηρίον
Εἰς ἀκρατῆ κίνησιν ἠρεθισμένον,
Τῇ δὲ προσηνὲς καὶ θρασύτητος ξένον.
Καὶ πῇ μὲν αὐτῶν ἀκροᾶσθαι τῶν λόγων
Οὓς ἄν τις Ἰνδὸς εὖ τιθασεύων λέγοι,
Πῇ δὲ πρὸς αὐτοὺς τοὺς νομεῖς ἐπιτρέχειν
Εἰς τὰς παλαιὰς ἐκτραπὲν κακουργίας.
PHILE, *Expos. de Eleph.* l. 126, &c.

[2] Captain YULE, in his *Narrative of an Embassy to Ava in* 1855, records an illustration of this tendency of the elephant to sudden death; one newly captured, the process of taming which was exhibited to the British Envoy, "made vigorous resistance to the placing of a collar on its neck, and the people were proceeding to tighten it, when the elephant, which had lain down as if quite exhausted, reared suddenly on the hind quarters, and fell on its side—*dead!*" (P. 104.)

Mr. STRACHAN noticed the same liability of the elephants to sudden death from very slight causes; "if they fall," he says, "at any time, though on plain ground, they either die immediately, or languish till they die; their great weight occasioning them so much hurt by the fall." (*Phil. Trans.* A.D. 1701, vol. xxiii. p. 1052.)

The first employment to which an elephant is put is to tread clay in a brick-field, or to draw a waggon in double harness with a tame companion. But the work in which the display of sagacity renders his labour of the highest value, is that which involves the moving of heavy materials; and hence in dragging and piling timber, or conveying stones[1] for the construction of retaining walls and the approaches to bridges his services in an unopened country are of the utmost importance. When roads are to be constructed along the face of steep declivities, and the space is so contracted that risk is incurred either of the working elephant falling over the precipice or of rocks slipping down from above, not only are the measures to which he resorts the most judicious and reasonable that could be devised, but if urged by his keeper to adopt any other, he manifests a reluctance sufficient to show that he has balanced in his own mind the comparative advantages of each. An elephant appears on all occasions to comprehend the purpose and object that he is expected to promote, and hence he voluntarily executes a variety of details without any guidance whatever from his keeper. This is one characteristic in which this animal manifests a superiority over the horse; although an elephant's strength in proportion to its weight is not so great as that of the latter.

His minute motions when engrossed by such operations, the activity of his eye, and the earnestness of his

[1] A correspondent informs me that on the Malabar coast of India, the elephant, when employed in dragging stones, moves them by means of a rope, which he either draws with his forehead, or manages by seizing it in his teeth.

attitudes, can only be comprehended by being seen. In moving timber and masses of rock his trunk is the instrument on which he mainly relies, but those which have tusks turn them to good account. To get a weighty stone out of a hollow an elephant will kneel down so as to apply the pressure of his head to move it upwards, then steadying it with one foot till he can raise himself, he will apply a fold of his trunk to shift it to its place, and fit it accurately in position : this done, he will step round to view it on either side, and adjust it with due precision. He appears to gauge his task by his eye, and to form a judgment whether the weight be proportionate to his strength. If doubtful of his own power, he hesitates and halts, and if urged against his will, he roars and shows temper.

In clearing an opening through forest land, the power of the African elephant, and the strength ascribed to him by a recent traveller, as displayed in uprooting trees, have never been equalled or approached by anything I have seen of the elephant in Ceylon [1] or heard of them in India.

[1] "Here the trees were large and handsome, but not strong enough to resist the inconceivable strength of the mighty monarch of these forests ; almost every tree had half its branches broken short by them, and at every hundred yards I came upon entire trees, and these, *the largest in the forest*, uprooted clean out of the ground, and *broken short across their stems.*" (*A Hunter's Life in South Africa.* By R. GORDON CUMMING, vol. ii. p. 305.) "Spreading out from one another, they smash and destroy all the finest trees in the forest which happen to be in their course. . . . I have rode through forests where the trees thus broken lay so thick across one another, that it was almost impossible to ride through the districts." (*Ibid.* p. 310.)

Mr. Gordon Cumming does not name the trees which he saw thus "uprooted" and "broken across," nor has he given any idea of their size and weight ; but Major DENHAM, who observed like traces of the elephant in Africa, saw only small trees overthrown by them ; and Mr. PRINGLE, who had an opportunity of observing similar practices of the animals in the neutral territory of the Eastern frontier of the Cape of Good Hope, describes their ravages as

Of course much must depend on the nature of the timber and the moisture of the soil : thus a strong tree on the verge of a swamp may be overthrown with greater ease than a small and low one in parched and solid ground. I have seen no "tree" deserving the name, nothing but jungle and brushwood, thrown down by the mere movement of an elephant without some special exertion of force. But he is by no means fond of gratuitously tasking his strength; and food being so abundant that he obtains it without an effort, it is not altogether apparent, even were he able to do so, why he should assail "the largest trees in the forest," and encumber his own haunts with their broken stems; especially as there is scarcely anything which an elephant dislikes more than venturing amongst fallen timber.

A tree of twelve inches in diameter resisted successfully the most strenuous struggles of the largest elephant I ever saw led to it; and when directed by their keepers to clear away jungle, the removal of even a small tree or a healthy young coco-nut palm is a matter both of time and

being confined to the mimosas, "immense numbers of which had been torn out of the ground, and placed in an inverted position, in order to enable the animals to browse at their ease on the soft and juicy roots, which form a favourite part of their food. Many of the *larger mimosas had resisted all their efforts; and indeed it is only after heavy rain, when the soil is soft and loose, that they ever successfully attempt this operation.*" (PRINGLE'S *Sketches of South Africa.*) Sir S. BAKER, whose observation confirms my own, as to the limited dimensions of the trees overthrown by elephants in Ceylon, says that in the vicinity of the White Nile, where the principal food of the elephant is the mimosa, he saw trees uprooted by them, which measured 30 feet high and 4 feet 6 inches in diameter. But he is "convinced that no single elephant could have overturned them; and the natives assured him that they mutually assist one another, and that several engage together in the work of overthrowing a large tree; the powerful tushes of some being applied as crowbars in the roots while others pull at the branches their trunks." (*The Albert Nyanz* vol. i. p. 276.)

exertion. Hence the services of an elephant are of much less value in clearing a forest than in dragging and piling felled timber. But in the latter occupation he manifests an intelligence and dexterity which is surprising to a stranger, because the sameness of the operation enables the animal to go on for hours disposing of log after log, almost without a hint or direction from his attendant. For example, two elephants employed in piling ebony and satinwood in the yards attached to the commissariat stores at Colombo, were so accustomed to their work, that they were able to accomplish it with equal precision and with greater rapidity than if it had been done by dock-labourers. When the pile attained a certain height, and they were no longer able by their conjoint efforts to raise one of the heavy logs of ebony to the summit, they had been taught to lean two pieces against the heap, up the incline of which they gently rolled the remaining logs, and placed them trimly on the top.

It has been asserted that in their occupations "elephants are to a surprising extent the creatures of habit,"[1] that their movements are altogether mechanical, and that "they are annoyed by any deviation from their accustomed practice, and resent any constrained departure from the regularity of their course." So far as my own observation goes, this is incorrect; and I am assured by officers of experience, that in regard to changing his treatment, his hours or his occupation, an elephant requires no more consideration than a horse, but exhibits the same pliancy and facility.

[1] *Menageries, etc.* "The Elephant," vol. ii. p. 23.

At one point, however, the utility of the elephant stops short. Such is the intelligence and earnestness he displays in work, which he seems to conduct almost without supervision, that it has been assumed[1] that he would continue his labour, and accomplish his given task, as well in the absence of his keeper as during his presence. But here his innate love of ease displays itself, and if the eye of his attendant be withdrawn, the moment he has finished the thing immediately in hand, he will stroll away lazily, to browse or enjoy the luxury of fanning himself and blowing dust over his back.

The means of punishing so powerful an animal is a question of difficulty to his attendants. Force being almost inapplicable, they try to work on his passions and feelings, by such expedients as altering the nature of his food or withholding it altogether for a time. On such occasions the demeanour of the creature will sometimes evince a sense of humiliation as well as of discontent. In some parts of India it is customary, in dealing with offenders, to stop their allowance of sugar canes or of jaggery; or to restrain them from eating their own share of fodder and leaves till their companions shall have finished; and in such cases the consciousness of degradation, betrayed by the looks and attitudes of the culprit, is quite sufficient to identify him, and to excite a feeling of sympathy and commiseration.

The elephant's obedience to his keeper is the result of affection, as well as of fear; and although his attachment becomes so strong that an elephant in Ceylon has been

[1] *Menageries, etc.* ch. vi. p. 130.

known to remain out all night, without food, rather than abandon his mahout, lying intoxicated in the jungle, yet he manifests little difficulty in yielding the same submission to a new driver in the event of a change of attendants. This is opposed to the popular belief that "the elephant cherishes such an enduring remembrance of his old mahout, that he cannot easily be brought to obey a stranger." [1] In the extensive establishments of the Ceylon Government, the keepers are changed without hesitation, and the animals, when equally kindly treated, are usually found to be as tractable and obedient to their new driver as to the old, so soon as they have become familiarised with his voice.

This is not, however, invariably the case; and Mr. CRIPPS, who had remarkable opportunities for observing the habits of the elephant in Ceylon, mentioned to me an instance in which one of a singularly stubborn disposition occasioned some inconvenience after the death of its keeper, by refusing to obey any other, till its attendants bethought them of a child about twelve years old, in a distant village, where the animal had been formerly picketed, and to whom it had displayed much attachment. The child was sent for; and on its arrival the elephant, as anticipated, manifested extreme satisfaction, and was managed with ease, till by degrees it became reconciled to the presence of a new superintendent.

It has been said that the mahouts die young, owing to some supposed injury to the spinal column from the peculiar motion of the elephant; but this remark does not

[1] *Menageries, etc.* "The Elephant," vol. i. p. 19.

apply to those in Ceylon, who are healthy, and as long-lived as other men. If the motion of the elephant be thus injurious, that of the camel must be still more so; yet we never hear of early death ascribed to this cause by the Arabs.

The voice of the keeper, with a very limited vocabulary of articulate sounds, serves almost alone to guide the elephant in his domestic occupations.[1] Sir EVERARD HOME, from an examination of the muscular fibres in the drum of an elephant's ear, came to the conclusion, that notwithstanding the distinctness and power of his perception of sounds at a greater distance than other animals, he was insensible to their harmonious modulation and destitute of a musical ear.[2] But Professor HARRISON, in a paper read before the Royal Irish

[1] The principal sound by which the mahouts in Ceylon direct the motions of the elephants is a repetition, with various modulations, of the words *ur-re! ur-re!* This is one of those interjections in which the sound is so expressive of the sense that persons in charge of animals of almost every description throughout the world appear to have adopted it with a concurrence that is very curious. The drivers of camels in Turkey, Palestine, and Egypt encourage them to speed by shouting *ar-ré! ar-ré!* The Arabs in Algeria cry *eirich!* to their mules. The Moors seem to have carried the custom with them into Spain, where mules are still driven with cries of *arré* (whence the muleteers derive their Spanish appellation of "arrieros"). In France the sportsman excites the hound by shouts of *hare! hare!* and the waggoner there turns his horses by his voice, and the use of the word *hurhaut!* In the North, "*Hurs* was a word used by the old Germans in urging their horses to speed;" and Sir FRANCIS HEAD, in his *Bubbles from the Brunnens*, describes the Schwin-General shouting "*ariff*" to his pigs —"*ariff!* vociferated the old man, striding after one of his rebellious subjects; *ariff!* re-echoed his boy striding after another." (P. 94.)

To the present day, the herdsmen in Ireland, and parts of Scotland, drive their pigs with shouts of *hurrish!* a sound closely resembling that used by the mahouts in Ceylon.

[2] *On the Difference between the Human Membrana tympani and that of the Elephant.* By Sir EVERARD HOME, Bart., *Philos. Trans.* 1823. Paper by Prof. HARRISON, *Proc. Royal Irish Academy*, vol. iii. p. 386.

Academy in 1847, has stated that on a careful examination of the head of an elephant which he had dissected, he could "see no evidence of the muscular structure of the *membrana tympani* so accurately described by Sir E. HOME." Sir EVERARD'S deduction, I may observe, is clearly inconsistent with the fact that the power of two elephants may be combined by singing to them a measured chant, somewhat resembling a sailor's capstan song; and in labour of a particular kind, such as hauling a stone with ropes, they will thus move conjointly a weight to which their divided strength would be unequal.[1]

Nothing can more strongly exhibit the impulse to obedience in the elephant, than the patience with which, at the order of his keeper, he swallows the nauseous medicines of the native elephant-doctors; and it is impossible to witness the fortitude with which, without shrinking, he submits to excruciating surgical operations for the removal of tumours and ulcers, without conceiving a vivid impression of his gentleness and intelligence. Dr. DAVY when in Ceylon was consulted about

[1] I have already noticed the striking effect produced on the captive elephants in the corral, by the harmonious notes of an ivory flute; and on looking to the graphic description which is given by ÆLIAN of the exploits which he witnessed as performed by the elephants exhibited at Rome, it is remarkable how very large a share of their training appears to have been ascribed to the employment of music.

PHILE, in the account which he has given of the elephant's fondness for music, would almost seem to have versified the prose narrative of ÆLIAN, as he describes its excitement at the more animated portions, its step being regulated to the time and movements of the harmony: the whole "*surprising in a creature whose limbs are without joints!*"

Καινόν τι ποιῶν ἐξ ἀνάρθρων ὀργάνων.

PHILE, *Expos. de Eleph.* l. 216.

For an account of the training and performances of the elephants at Rome, as narrated by ÆLIAN, see the appendix to this chapter.

an elephant in the Government stud, which was suffering from a deep, burrowing sore in the back, just over the back-bone, and this had long resisted the treatment ordinarily employed. He recommended the use of the knife, that vent might be given to the accumulated matter, but no one of the attendants was competent to undertake the operation. "Being assured," he continues, "that the creature would behave well, I undertook it myself. The elephant was not bound, but was made to kneel down at his keeper's command—and with an amputating knife, using all my force, I made the incision required through the tough integuments. The elephant did not flinch, but rather inclined towards me when using the knife ; and merely uttered a low, and as it were suppressed, groan. In short, he behaved as like a human being as possible, as if conscious (as I believe he was), that the operation was for his good, and the pain unavoidable." [1]

Obedience to the orders of his keepers is not, however, to be assumed as the result of a uniform perception of the object to be attained by compliance ; and we cannot but remember the touching incident which took place during the slaughter of the elephant at Exeter Change in 1826, when, after receiving ineffectually upwards of 120 balls in various parts of his body, he turned his face to his assailants on hearing the voice of

[1] *The Angler in the Lake District*, p. 23. A similar story is told in the *Memoir of Bishop Wilson*, of an elephant which when suffering with ophthalmia had experienced the relief derived from a solution of nitrate of silver, and voluntarily offered its eye for a re-application of the remedy, on a second visit of the surgeon.

his keeper, and knelt down at the accustomed word of command, so as to bring his forehead within view of the rifles.[1]

The working elephant is always a delicate animal, and requires watchfulness and care. As a beast of burden it is unsatisfactory; for although in point of mere strength there is scarcely any weight which could be conveniently placed on it that it could not carry, it is difficult to pack the load without causing abrasions that afterwards ulcerate. The skin is easily chafed by harness, especially in wet weather. During either long droughts or too much moisture, an elephant's feet become liable to sores, that render it non-effective for months. Many attempts have been made to provide some protection for the sole of the foot, but from the extreme weight and the peculiar mode of planting the foot, they have all been unsuccessful. The eyes are also liable to frequent inflammations, and the skill of the native elephant-doctors, which has been renowned since the time of Ælian, is nowhere more strikingly displayed than in the successful treatment of such attacks.[2] In Ceylon, the murrain among the cattle is of frequent occurrence, and carries off great numbers of animals, wild as well as tame. In such visitations the elephants suffer severely, not only those at liberty in the forest, but those carefully tended in the Government stables. Out of a stud of about 40 attached to the department of the Commission of Roads, the deaths between 1841 and

[1] A shocking account of the death of this poor animal is given in HONE'S *Every-Day Book*, March 1830, p. 337.

[2] ÆLIAN, lib. xiii. c. 7.

1849 were on an average *four* in each year, and this was nearly doubled in those years when murrain prevailed.

Of 240 elephants, employed in the public departments of the Ceylon Government, which died in twenty-five years, from 1831 to 1856, the length of time that each lived in captivity has only been recorded in the instances of 138. Of these there died :—

Duration of Captivity	No.	Male	Female
Under 1 year	72	29	43
From 1 to 2 years . .	14	5	9
" 2 " 3 " . .	8	5	3
" 3 " 4 " . .	8	3	5
" 4 " 5 " . .	3	2	1
" 5 " 6 " . .	2	2	.
" 6 " 7 " . .	3	1	2
" 7 " 8 " . .	5	2	3
" 8 " 9 " . .	5	5	.
" 9 " 10 " . .	2	2	.
" 10 " 11 " . .	2	2	.
" 11 " 12 " . .	3	1	2
" 12 " 13 " . .	3	.	3
" 13 " 14 " . .	.	.	.
" 14 " 15 " . .	3	1	2
" 15 " 16 " . .	1	1	.
" 16 " 17 " . .	1	.	1
" 17 " 18 " . .	.	.	.
" 18 " 19 " . .	2	1	1
" 19 " 20 " . .	1	.	1
Total . .	138	62	76

Of the 72 who died in one year's servitude, 35 expired within the first six months of their captivity. During training, many elephants die in the unaccountable manner already referred to, of what the natives designate a *broken heart.*

On being first subjected to work, the elephant is liable to severe and often fatal swellings of the jaws and abdomen.[1]

From these causes there died, between 1841 and 1849	9
Of cattle murrain	10
Sore feet	1
Colds and inflammation	6
Diarrhœa	1
Worms	1
Of diseased liver	1
Injuries from a fall	1
General debility	1
Unknown causes	3

Of the entire, twenty-three were females and eleven males.

The ages of those that died could not be accurately stated, owing to the circumstance of their having been captured in corral. Two only were tuskers. Towards keeping the stud in health, nothing has been found so conducive as regularly bathing the elephants, and giving them the opportunity to stand with their feet in water, or in moistened earth.

Elephants are said to be afflicted with tooth-ache; their tushes have likewise been found with symptoms of internal perforation by some parasite, and the natives assert that, in their agony, the animals have been known to break them off short.[2] I have never heard of the teeth themselves being so affected, and it is just possible that the operation of shedding and the subsequent

[1] The elephant which was dissected by Dr. HARRISON of Dublin, in 1847, died of a febrile attack, after four or five days' illness, which, as Dr. H. tells me in a private letter, was "very like scarlatina, at that time a prevailing disease: its skin in some places became almost scarlet."

[2] See a paper, entitled "*Recollections of Ceylon*," in *Fraser's Magazine* for December 1860.

decay of the milk-tushes, may have in some instances been accompanied by incidents that gave rise to this story. At the same time the probabilities are in favour of its being true. CUVIER committed himself to the statement that the tusks of the elephant have no attachments to connect them with the pulp lodged in the cavity at their base, from which the peculiar modification of dentine, known as "ivory" is secreted;[1] and hence, by inference, that they would be devoid of sensation. But independently of the fact that ivory is permeated by tubes so fine that at their origin from the pulpy cavity they do not exceed the $\frac{1}{15000}$ part of an inch in diameter, OWEN had the tusk and pulp of the great elephant which died at the Zoological Gardens in London in 1847 longitudinally divided, and found that, "although the pulp could be easily detached from the inner surface of the cavity, it was not without a certain resistance; and when the edges of the co-adapted pulp and tusk were examined by a strong lens, the filamentary processes from the outer surface of the former could be seen stretching, as they were drawn from the dentinal tubes, before they broke. These filaments are so minute, he adds, that to the naked eye the detached surface of the pulp seems to be entire; and hence CUVIER was deceived into supposing that there was no organic connexion between the pulp and the ivory. But if, as there seems no reason to doubt, these delicate

[1] *Annales du Muséum*, F. viii. 1805. p. 94, and *Ossemens Fossiles*, quoted by OWEN, in the article on "Teeth," in TODD's *Cyclop. of Anatomy, etc.* vol. iv. p. 929.

nervous processes traverse the tusk by means of the numerous tubes already described, if attacked by caries the pain occasioned to the elephant would be excruciating.

As to maintaining a stud of elephants for the purposes to which they are now assigned in Ceylon, there may be a question on the score of prudence and economy. In the wild and unopened parts of the country, where rivers are to be forded, and forests are only traversed by jungle paths, their labour is of value, in certain contingencies, in the conveyance of stores, and in the earlier operations for the construction of fords and rough bridges of timber. But in more highly civilised districts, and wherever macadamised roads admit of the employment of horses and oxen for draught, I apprehend that the services of the elephant might, with advantage, be gradually reduced, if not altogether dispensed with.

The love of the elephant for coolness and shade renders it at all times more or less impatient of work in the sun, and every moment of leisure it can snatch is employed in covering its back with dust, or fanning itself to diminish the annoyance of the insects and heat. From the tenderness of the skin and its liability to sores, the labour in which the elephant can most advantageously be employed is that of draught; but the reluctance of horses to meet or pass them renders it difficult to work them with safety on frequented roads. Besides, were the full load which an elephant is capable of drawing, proportionally to its muscular strength, to be placed upon waggons of corresponding dimension, the injury to roads from the extra weight would be such that the wear and tear of the highways and bridges would prove too costly to be borne. On the other hand, by restricting it to a somewhat more manageable quantity, and by limiting the weight, as at present, to about *one ton and a half*, it is doubtful whether an elephant performs so much more work than could be done by a horse or by bullocks, as to compensate for the greater cost of his feeding and attendance.

Add to this, that from accidents and other causes, from ulcerations of the skin, and illnesses of many kinds, the elephant is so often invalided, that the actual cost of its labour, when at work, is very considerably enhanced. Exclusive of the salaries of higher officers attached to the Government establishments, and other permanent charges, the expenses of an elephant, looking only to the wages of its attendants and the cost of its food and medicines, varies from *three shillings to four shillings and sixpence* per diem, according to its size and class.[1] Taking the average at three shillings and nine-

[1] An ordinary-sized elephant engrosses the undivided attention of *three* men. One, as his mahout or superintendent, and two as leaf-cutters, who bring him branches and grass for his daily supplies. An animal of larger growth would probably require a third leaf-cutter. The daily consumption is two cwt. of green food with about half a bushel of grain. When in the vicinity of towns and villages, the attendants have no difficulty in procuring an abundant supply of the branches of the trees to which elephants are partial; and in journeys through the forests and unopened country, the leaf-cutters are sufficiently expert in the knowledge of those particular plants with which the elephant is satisfied. Those that would be likely to disagree with him he unerringly rejects. His favourites are the palms, especially the cluster of rich, unopened leaves, known as the "cabbage," of the coco-nut and areca; and he delights to tear open the young trunks of the palmyra and jaggery (*Caryota urens*) in search of the farinaceous matter contained in the spongy pith. Next to these come the varieties of fig-trees, particularly the sacred *Bo*

pence, and calculating that hardly any individual works more than four days out of seven, the charge for each day so employed would amount to *six shillings and sixpence.* The keep per day of a powerful dray-horse, working five days in the week, would not exceed half-a-crown, and two such would unquestionably do more work than any elephant under the present system. I do not know whether it be from a comparative calculation of this kind that the strength of the elephant establishments in Ceylon has been gradually diminished of late years, but in the department of the Commissioner of Roads, the stud, which formerly numbered upwards of sixty elephants, was reduced, some years ago, to thirty-six, and is at present less than half that number.

The fallacy of the supposed reluctance of the elephant to breed in captivity has been demonstrated by many recent authorities; but with the exception of the birth of young elephants at Rome, as mentioned by ÆLIAN,

(*F. religiosa*) which is found near every temple, and the *na gaha* (*Messua ferrea*), with thick dark leaves and a scarlet flower. The leaves of the jak-tree and bread-fruit (*Artocarpus integrifolia*, and *A. incisa*), the wood apple (*Ægle Marmelos*), Palu (*Mimusops Indica*), and a number of others well known to their attendants, are all consumed in turn. The stems of the plaintain, the stalks of the sugar-cane, and the feathery tops of the bamboos, are irresistible luxuries. Pine-apples, water-melons, and fruits of every description, are voraciously devoured, and a coconut when found is first rolled under foot to detach it from the husk and fibre, and then raised in his trunk and crushed almost without an effort, by his ponderous jaws.

The grasses are not found in sufficient quantity to be an item of daily fodder; the Mauritius or the Guinea grass is seized with avidity; lemon grass is rejected from its overpowering perfume, but rice in the straw, and every description of grain, whether growing or dry; gram (*Cicer arietinum*), Indian corn, and millet, are his natural food. Of such of these as can be found, it is the duty of the leaf-cutters, when in the jungle and on march, to provide a daily supply.

the only instances that I am aware of their actually producing young under such circumstances, took place in Ceylon. Both parents had been for several years attached to the stud of the Commissioner of Roads, and in 1844 the female, whilst engaged in dragging a waggon, gave birth to a still-born calf. Some years before, an elephant that had been captured by Mr. Cripps, dropped a female calf, which he succeeded in rearing. As usual, the little one became the pet of the keepers; but as it increased in growth, it exhibited the utmost violence when thwarted; striking out with its hind-feet, throwing itself headlong on the ground, and pressing its trunk against any opposing object.

The duration of life in the elephant has been from the remotest times a matter of uncertainty and speculation. Aristotle says it was reputed to live from two to three hundred years,[1] and modern zoologists have assigned to it an age very little less; CUVIER[2] allots two hundred and DE BLAINVILLE[3] one hundred and twenty. The only attempt which I know of to establish a period historically or physiologically is that of FLEURENS, who has advanced an ingenious theory on the subject in his treatise "*De la Longévité Humaine.*" He assumes the sum total of life in all animals to be equivalent to five times the number of years requisite to perfect their growth and development;—and he adopts as evidence of the period at which growth ceases, the final consolidation of the bones with their *epiphyses*; which in the

[1] ARISTOTELES *de Anim.* l. viii. c. 9.

[2] *Ménag. de Mus. Nat.* p. 107.

[3] *Ostéographie*, "Eléph." p. 74

young consist of cartilages; but in the adult become uniformly osseous and solid. So long as the epiphyses are distinct from the bones, the growth of the animal is proceeding, but it ceases so soon as the consolidation is complete. In man, according to FLEURENS, this consummation takes place at 20 years of age, in the horse at 5, in the dog at 2; so that conformably to this theory the respective normal age for each would be 100 years for man, 25 for the horse, and 10 for a dog. As a datum for his conclusion, FLEURENS cites the instance of one young elephant in which, at 26 years old, the epiphyses were still distinct, whereas in another, which died at 31, they were firm and adherent. Hence he draws the inference that the period of completed solidification is thirty years, and consequently that the normal age of the elephant is *one hundred and fifty.*[1]

Amongst the Singhalese the ancient fable of the elephant attaining to the age of two or three hundred years still prevails; but the Europeans, and those in immediate charge of tame ones, entertain the opinion that the duration of life for about *seventy* years is common both to man and the elephant; and that before the arrival of the latter period, symptoms of debility and decay ordinarily begin to manifest themselves. Still instances are not wanting in Ceylon of trained decoys that have lived for more than double the reputed period in actual servitude. One employed by Mr. Cripps in the Seven Korles was represented by the cooroowe people to have served the king of Kandy in the same capacity sixty

[1] FLEURENS, *De la Longévité Humaine*, pp. 82, 89.

years before; and amongst the papers left by Colonel Robertson (son to the historian of "Charles V."), who held a command in Ceylon in 1799, shortly after the capture of the island by the British, I have found a memorandum showing that a decoy was then attached to the elephant establishment at Matura, which the records proved to have served under the Dutch during the entire period of their occupation (extending to upwards of one hundred and forty years); and it was said to have been found in the stables by the Dutch on the expulsion of the Portuguese in 1656.

It is perhaps from this popular belief in their almost illimitable age, that the natives generally assert that the body of a dead elephant is seldom or never to be discovered in the woods. And certain it is that frequenters of the forest with whom I have conversed, whether European or Singhalese, are consistent in their assurances that they have never found the remains of an elephant that had died a natural death. One chief, the Wannyah of the Trincomalie district, told a friend of mine, that once after a severe murrain, which had swept the province, he found the carcasses of elephants that had died of the disease. On the other hand, a European gentleman, who for thirty-six years without intermission has been living in the jungle, ascending to the summits of mountains in the prosecution of the trigonometrical survey, and penetrating valleys in tracing roads and opening means of communication,—one, too, who has made the habits of the wild elephant a subject of constant observation and study,—has often expressed to me his astonishment that after seeing many thousands of living elephants in all possible situations, he had never yet found a single skeleton of a dead one, except of those which had fallen by the rifle.[1]

It has been suggested that the bones of the elephant may be so porous and spongy as to disappear in consequence of an early decomposition; but this remark would not apply to the grinders or to the tusks; besides which, the inference is at variance with the fact, that not only the horns and teeth, but entire skeletons of deer, are frequently found in the districts inhabited by the elephant.

The natives, to account for this popular belief, declare that the survivors of the herd bury such of their companions as die a natural death.[2] It is curious that this belief was current also amongst the Greeks of the Lower Empire; and PHILE, writing early in the fourteenth century, not only describes the younger elephants as tending the wounded, but as burying the dead:

Ὅταν δ' ἐπιστῇ τῆς τελευτῆς ὁ χρόνος
Κοινοῦ τέλους ἄμυναν ὁ ξένος φέρει.[3]

[1] This remark regarding the elephant of Ceylon does not appear to extend to that of Africa, as I observe that BEAVER, in his *African Memoranda*, says that "the skeletons of old ones that have died in the woods are frequently found." (*African Memoranda relative to an attempt to establish British Settlements at the Island of Bulama.* Lond. 1815, p. 353.)

[2] A corral was organised near Putlam in 1846, by Mr. Morris, the chief officer of the district. It was constructed across one of the paths to which the elephants resort in their frequent marches, and during the course of the proceedings two of the captured elephants died. Their carcases were left of course within the enclosure, which was abandoned as soon as the capture was complete. The wild elephants resumed their path through it, and a few days afterwards the headman reported to Mr. Morris that the bodies had been removed and carried outside the corral to a spot to which nothing but the elephants could have borne them.

[3] *Expositio de Eleph.* l. 243.

The Singhalese have a further superstition in relation to the close of life in the elephant: they believe that, on feeling the approach of dissolution, he repairs to a solitary valley, and there resigns himself to death. A native who accompanied Mr. Cripps, when hunting, in the forests of Anarajapoora, intimated to him that he was then in the immediate vicinity of the spot "*to which the elephants come to die*," but that it was so mysteriously concealed, that although every one believed in its existence, no one had ever succeeded in penetrating to it. At the corral which I have described at Kornegalle, in 1847, Dehigame, one of the Kandyan chiefs, assured me it was the universal belief of his countrymen, that the elephants, when about to die, resorted to a valley in Saffragam, among the mountains to the east of Adam's Peak, which was reached by a narrow pass with walls of rock on either side, and that there, by the side of a lake of clear water, they took their last repose.[1] It was not without interest that I afterwards recognised this tradition in the story of *Sinbad of the Sea*, who in his Seventh Voyage, after conveying the presents of Haroun al Raschid to the king of Serendib, is wrecked on his return from Ceylon, and sold as a slave to a master who employs him in shooting elephants for the sake of their

[1] The selection by animals of a *place to die*, is not confined to the elephant. DARWIN says, that in South America "the guanacos (llamas) appear to have favourite spots for lying down to die; on the banks of the Santa Cruz river, in certain circumscribed spaces which were generally bushy and all near the water, the ground was actually white with their bones: on one such spot I counted between ten and twenty heads."—*Nat. Voy.* ch. viii. The same has been remarked in the Rio Gallegos; and at St. Jago in the Cape de Verde Islands, DARWIN saw a retired corner similarly covered with the bones of the goat, as if it were "the burial-ground of all the goats in the island."

ivory; till one day the tree on which he was stationed having been uprooted by one of the herd, he fell senseless to the ground, and the great elephant approaching wound his trunk around him and carried him away, ceasing not to proceed until he had taken him to a place where, his terror having subsided, *he found himself amongst the bones of elephants, and knew that this was their burial place.*[1] It is curious to find this legend of Ceylon in what has, not inaptly, been described as the "Arabian Odyssey" of Sinbad; the original of which evidently embodies the romantic recitals of the sailors returning from the navigation of the Indian Seas, in the middle ages,[2] which were current amongst the Mussulmans, and are reproduced in various forms throughout the tales of the *Arabian Nights.*

[1] *Arabian Nights' Entertainment*, LANE's edition, vol. iii. p. 77.

[2] See a disquisition on the origin of the story of Sinbad, by M. REINAUD, in the introduction prefixed to his translation of the *Arabian Geography of Aboulfeda*, vol. i. p. lxxvi.

APPENDIX TO CHAPTER III.

As Ælian's work on *the Nature of Animals* has never, I believe, been republished in any English version, and the passage in relation to the training and performance of elephants is so pertinent to the present inquiry, I venture to subjoin a translation of the 11th chapter of his 2nd book.

"Of the cleverness of the elephant I have spoken elsewhere, and likewise of the manner of hunting. I have mentioned these things, a few out of the many which others have stated; but for the present I purpose to speak of their musical feeling, their tractability, and facility in learning what it is difficult for even a human being to acquire, much less a beast, hitherto so wild:—such as to dance, as is done on the stage; to walk with a measured gait; to listen to the melody of the flute and to perceive the difference of sounds, that, being pitched low lead to a slow movement, or high to a quick one; all this the elephant learns and understands, and is accurate withal, and makes no mistake. Thus has Nature formed him not only the greatest in size, but the most gentle and the most easily taught. Now if I were going to write about the tractability and aptitude to learn amongst those of India, Æthiopia, and Libya, I should probably appear to be concocting a tale and acting the braggart, or to be telling a falsehood respecting the nature of the animal founded on a mere report, all which it behoves a philosopher, and most of all one who is an ardent lover of truth, not to do. But what I have seen myself, and what others have described as having occurred at Rome, this I have chosen to relate, selecting a few facts out of many, to show the particular nature of those creatures. The elephant when tamed is an animal most gentle and most easily led to do whatever he is directed. And by way of showing honour to time, I will first narrate events of the oldest date. Cæsar Germanicus, the nephew of Tiberius, exhibited once a public show, wherein there were many full-grown elephants, male and female, and some of their breed born in this country. When their limbs were beginning to become firm, a person familiar with such animals instructed them by a strange and surpassing method of teaching; using only gentleness and kindness, and adding to his mild lessons the bait of pleasant and varied food. By this means he led them by degrees to throw off all wildness, and, as it were, to desert to a state of civilisation, conducting themselves in a manner almost human. He taught them neither to be excited on hearing the pipe, nor to be disturbed by the beat of drum, but to be soothed by the sounds of the reed, and to endure unmusical noises and the clatter of feet from persons while marching; and they were trained to feel no fear of a mass of men, nor to be enraged at the infliction of blows, not even when compelled to twist their limbs and to bend them like a stage dancer, and this too although endowed with strength and might. And there is in this a very noble addition to nature, not to conduct themselves in a disorderly manner and disobediently towards the instructions of man; for after the dancing-master had made them expert, and they had learnt their lessons accurately, they did not belie the labour of his instruction whenever a necessity and opportunity called upon them to exhibit what they had been taught. For the whole troop came forward from this and that side of the theatre, and divided themselves into parties; they advanced walking with a mincing gait and exhibiting in their whole body and persons the manners of a beau, clothed in the flowery dresses of dancers; and on the ballet-master giving a signal with his voice, they fell into line and went round in a circle, and if it were requisite to deploy they did so. They ornamented the floor of the stage by throwing flowers upon it, and this they did in moderation and sparingly, and straightway they beat a measure with their feet and kept time together.

"Now that Damon and Spintharus and Aristoxenus and Xenophilus and Philoxenus and others should know music excellently well, and for their cleverness be ranked amongst the few, is indeed a thing of wonder, but not incredible nor contrary at all to reason. For this reason, that a *man* is a rational animal, and the recipient of mind and intelligence. But that a jointless animal (*ἄναρθρον*) should understand rhythm and melody, and preserve a gesture, and not deviate from a measured movement, and fulfil the requirements of those who laid down instructions, these are gifts of nature, I think, and a peculiarity in every way astounding. Added to these there were things enough to drive the spectator out of his senses; when the strewn rushes and other materials for beds on the ground were placed on the sand of the theatre, and they received stuffed mattresses such as belonged to rich houses, and variegated bed-coverings, and goblets were placed there very expensive, and bowls of gold and silver, and in them a great quantity of water; and tables were placed there of sweet-smelling wood and ivory very superb: and upon them flesh meats and loaves enough to fill the stomachs of animals the most voracious. When the preparations were completed and abundant, the banqueters came forward, six male and an equal number of female elephants ; the former had on a male dress and the latter a female; and on a signal being given they stretched forward their trunks in a subdued manner, and took their food in great moderation, and not one of them appeared to be gluttonous greedy, or to snatch at a greater portion, as did the Persian mentioned by Xenophon. And when it was requisite to drink, a bowl was placed by the side of each ; and inhaling with their trunks they took a draught very orderly; and then they scattered the drink about in fun; but not as in insult. Many other acts of a similar kind, both clever and astonishing, have persons described, relating to the peculiarities of these animals, and I saw them writing letters on Roman tablets with their trunks, neither looking awry nor turning aside. The hand, however, of the teacher was placed so as to be a guide in the formation of the letters; and while it was writing the animal kept its eye fixed down in an accomplished and scholarlike manner."

INDEX.

ADAM'S PEAK, ascent of by elephants, *page* 41
—, encounter with wild elephants near, 77
Adventures with elephants, 71
ÆLIAN, account of the export of elephants from Ceylon, 5 *n.*
— his fallacy as to the elephant shedding his tusks, 7 *n.*
— alleged antipathy of the elephant and rhinoceros, 9, 15
— his account of training, 151
— error as to the elephant being without joints, 34, 35 *n.*
— says elephants were trained to kill by their knees, 16 *n.*
— on the supposed superiority of the Ceylon to the Indian elephant, 152 *n.*
— elephant, love of music, 168 *n.*
— elephants performing at Rome, 168 *n.*, 183
Aetagalla Rock, legend of, 107
Affection for their young, 47
African elephant teeth different from Indian, vi.
— ribs and vertebræ, vi. vii. 20
— both sexes have tusks, 6
— ivory preferred to Ceylon in Europe, 6 *n.*
— conjecture respecting tusks, 7
— great size of tusks; 300 lbs. and upwards, 7, 8
African elephant is not vulnerable in the forehead, as the Ceylon elephant is, *page* 81
Age of elephants, 123, 177
— estimated duration of life in, 177
Airavanta, Sanscrit, origin of the word elephant, 4 *n.*
Alce. *See* Elk, 33
Alexandri Epistola ad Aristotelem, 11
Alexander the Great, his Indian expedition, 150
— coins of, 151 *n.*
Alisaunder, English romance of, 12 *n.*
Allia. *See* Hora allia, 82. *See* Rogue
Alligator River, elephant hunt at, 106
Anarajapoora, instinct exhibited by elephants at, 65
Anatomy of the elephant imperfectly known, 56
— account of by Molyneux, A.D. 1696, 56 *n.*
ANSTED, Prof., on the height of elephants, 31 *n.*
Antipater brought the first Indian elephant to Greece, 150
Antipathy of elephants to other animals, 12, 15
— its improbability, 15

Ants, superior to the elephant in sagacity, 68
— their marvellous power of discovering sugar, 139 *n.*
Arabian Nights, story of the burial place of dead elephants, 182
ἄρπη. *See* Hendoo, 156 *n.*
ARISTOTLE, on the trunk of the elephant, 28 *n.*
— on the fallacy of the elephant having no joints, 33
— on the double stomach of the elephant, 57 *n.*
— on its mode of levelling trees, 140 *n.*
ARMANDI, error as to the height of Ceylon elephant, 31 *n.*
— on the double stomach of, 67 *n.*
— on elephants in war, 151
Ar-ré, sound to guide elephants, 167 *n.*
— its variations in various countries, ib.
Arundel MSS., errors as to the elephant, 36
Assam, elephant of, x.
Avisavelle, elephant corral at, 43

BADULLA, fight between two elephants at, 16
— adventures with elephants near, 71, 74
BAKER, Sir SAMUEL, on the weight of African ivory, 8 *n.*
— his stories of elephant shooting, 77 *n.*
— on the difference between the Ceylon and African species, 20 *n.*
— on power to uproot trees, 162 *n.*
— on the size of the elephant's foot in Africa, 98 *n.*
BARBEZIEUX, RICHARD DE, error as to joints of elephant, 37
Bari, size of African ivory at, 8 *n.*
Bathing elephants, story of, 51, 55 *n.*
BENARY, his theory of the derivation of the word elephant, 4 *n.*
Bengal, elephants of, viii.
— method of poisoning them, 6
— mode of capturing them, 104
Bentinck, Baron, communication from, viii. ix.
BERNIER, as to the supposed superiority of the Ceylon elephant to that of India, 152
"*Bestiaries*" of the Middle Ages, in error as to the joints of the elephant, 36
Birmah, method of capturing elephants in, 97
Bison, its instinct as to harvest time, 64
BLAIR, Dr., on the anatomy of the elephant, 56 *n.*
BLES, M., affection of elephants for their young, 47. *See* Buffon
— on training elephants, 159 *n.*
Bo-trees, sacred; eaten by elephants, iii.
BOCHART, derivation of the word *elephant*, 4 *n.*
BONAPARTE, Prince LUCIEN, his account of the Sumatran elephant, vi.
Breeding in captivity, fallacy as to, 176
BRODERIP, on the mode of training, 155
— on the size of tusks in elephants, 8 *n.*
— on the stomach of, 56
BROOKE, Sir VICTOR, Bart., great elephant shot by, 9 *n.*
— immense tusk, 16
BROWNE, Sir THOMAS, *Vulgar Errors*, exposes the delusion as to there being no joints in the elephant, 32, 38
BUCHANAN, on rogue elephants, 49 *n.*
Buffalo, double stomach of, 63
BUFFON. *See* BLES

BUFFON, on the double stomach of the elephant, 57 *n.*
— on training, 159 *n.*
Burial place of the elephants, as told in the story of *Sinbad of the Sea*, 181
Burying their dead, alleged habit of elephants, 180

CÆSAR, his story of the *alce*, 33
Cambodia, method of training elephants in, 157
Camel, alleged antipathy of the elephant to, 13
— cellular stomach, 60
CAMPER, on the double stomach of the elephant, 58
Captivity, conduct of elephants when first taken, 150
Carthaginians employed elephants in war, 151
Caution of elephants as to pit-falls alleged, but doubtful, 67
Ceylon, geological formation of the island, vi.
— export of elephants to India, viii. 5
— profuse number of elephants in, 5
— cause of declining numbers, 6
Charlemagne, elephant sent to by Haroun Alraschid, 35
Chena cultivation, 64
China, Ceylon ivory preferred for carving, 62
Chittagong, elephant of, x.
Chuny, the tame elephant killed at Exeter Change, its cruel death, 169
Climbing, ability of the elephant in, 41
Cochin China, elephant of, xi.
COCKAYNE. See *Alexandri Epistola, etc.*, 11
Coco-nut, how eaten by an elephant, 64
COLERIDGE, on the sagacity of the elephant, 68
Colombo frequented by elephants in 1705 A.D., 5
COMBE, on the brain of the elephant, 86
Cooroowe. *See* Noosers, 122, 155
Coroners' inquests show few deaths by elephants, 10
Corral or Kraal, operations of, 95
— in Bengal, how constructed. *See* Keddah, 104
— dimensions, 113
— form of, 112
— its strength, 114
— the drive of the elephants, 115
— the rush and return, 116
— singular night scene, 117
— the capture made, 118
— noosed and secured, 121
— distress of the captives, and their struggles, 125, 135
— terror of the elephants for white rods, 128
— noticed by Pliny, 128, *n.*
— conduct of the young ones, 137
— extraordinary scene, 140
— interesting demeanour of the captives, 140
— a second herd driven in and taken, 143
— leading out the captives, 147
CORSE, his account of the Indian elephant, 47
COSMAS INDICOPLEUSTES, his account of the export of elephants from Ceylon, 5 *n.*
Courage in open ground, 86, 87
Cripps, Mr., description of a strange sound made by elephants, 29
— story of an elephant feigning death, 70
— on the taming and training of elephants, 158
— on their attachment to attendants, 166

Cripps, Mr., on elephants breeding in captivity, 177
Cruelties in elephant shooting, 77 *n.*
CTESIAS, fallacy that the elephant has no joints, 33
CUMMING, Mr. GORDON, his cruel experiments on the vital endurance of the elephant, 81 *n.*
— questionable stories of trees uprooted by elephants, 162 *n.*
Curiosity, spirit of, strong in the elephant, 67
— story of Colonel Hardy, 67
Cuspis. *See* Hendoo, 156 *n.*
Cuttack, elephant of, x.
— method of poisoning elephants in, 6
CUVIER, on the comparative sagacity of the elephant, 68
— on the tusks of elephants, 173
— on duration of life in, 177

DAH! DAH! word hateful to wild elephant, 100
Dakra, a poison for elephants in Bengal, 6
DARWIN, on the burial place of llamas and goats, 101 *n.*
DAVY, Dr., on endurance of pain in the elephant, 168
— on the spirit of curiosity in the elephant, 67
Dawson, Capt., an elephant shot by, dies standing, 39
DE BLAINVILLE, on the duration of life in the elephant, 177
DE BRY, story of a horse killed by a trained elephant, 13
Dead elephant, body rarely found, 179
Deafness occasional in elephants, 30
Death feigned by an elephant, 70
Decoy elephants, their conduct, 119, 123, 134
Défenses. *See* Tusks, 9
Dekkan, elephant of the, xi.
De Lima, General, immense tusks got by, in Africa, 8 *n.*
DENHAM, Major, on the height of an African elephant, 31
DENMAN, Major, power of elephant to overthrow trees, 162 *n.*
Descending acclivities, mode of, 44
Dentine, 173. *See* Ivory
DICUIL, description of the elephant of Charlemagne, 35
Dinka, size of African ivory at, 8, 12
DIODORUS SICULUS, on the sagacity of the Indian elephant, 150
Dogs, elephants impatient of, 14
— Major Skinner's dog, kept off the elephants by its bark, 15
— superior in sagacity to the elephant, 69
DONNE, his error as to the joints of the elephant, 38
Dublin, elephant burnt to death, 26 *n.*
"Duipa," an Indian name of the elephant, its signification, 62 *n.*
Dust, habit of throwing it over themselves, 133
Dutch possessions in India, vi. *See* Temminck
— elephant hunts conducted by, 95

EAR, formation of, 167
— love of music, 168 *n.*
— Sir EVERARD HOME, on hearing in the elephant, 167
Ebony, logs piled by elephants, 164
"Eleph," Hebrew, conjectured to be the root of elepha , 4 *n.*
"*Elephant*," derivation of the word, 4 *n.*
— conjectures of Pictet, Bochart, Pott, and Benary, 4 *n.*
— great numbers in Ceylon, 5

Elephant, will ere long be extinct in India, 6 *n.*
— alleged enmity to man, and other animals, 10
— signs of perfection in. See *Hastisilpe*, 21
— natural colour of the skin, 22
— loves shade, 25
— scene, by night while bathing, 52
— stomach of the elephant double, 56
— the Ceylon elephant supposed to exceed that of India in sagacity, 152
Elephant, the first brought to Greece by Antipater, 150
Elephant shooting. *See* Shooting
ἐλέφας signified not the elephant, but its *ivory*, 4 *n.*
— Benary's derivation of the word, 66
Elephas Sumatranus. *See* Sumatra, vi.
— supposed to differ from the elephant of India, vii.
— this theory doubted by Dr. Falconer, ix.
Elk, error of Cæsar in saying that the "alce" has no joints, 33
Englishman, Voyage of a certain, story of an elephant killing a horse, 13 *n.*
EVELYN, JOHN, refutes the fallacy that the elephant has no joints, 33
Eye of the elephant small, 26, ib. *n.*
— its accuracy when engaged in working, 261

FAIRHOLME on the elephant, 159 *n.*
FALCONER, Dr., doubts the alleged difference between the elephants of Sumatra and India, ix.
— on the height of elephants, 31 *n.*
Fanning themselves, habit of, 84
— extreme grace of the movement, 136
— in the corral, 135
Feet, habit of swinging, 84
— not, as supposed, a substitute for exercise, 85
Females in a herd, numerous, 47
Fences, elephant's dread of, 65
Filsben, Danish for ivory, 4 *n.*
Flesh of the elephant coarse, 88
FLEURENS, on the duration of life in the elephant, 177
Flies, their marvellous faculty of discerning carrion, 139 *n.*
— account of their hurrying to death-beds, 139 *n.*
Food of the elephant when wild, 63
when tamed and trained, 175
Foot, a frequent seat of disease, 170
— its extreme sensitiveness, 133
— of the elephant makes good soup, 89
— twice its circumference equal to the height of the animal, 98 *n.*
FORBES, ancedote from his *Oriental Memoirs*, 107 *n.*
Forehead of the elephant, wound in, fatal, 80
Fossil elephant, 159 *n.*
Fretz, Gerard, frightful wound, 90

GADJAH. *See* Sumatran elephant, vi.
Gallwey, Capt. P. Payne, number of elephants shot by him, 77 *n.*
Geological formation of Ceylon, vi.
"*Goondah.*" *See* Rogue, 48
Gooneratné Modliar, his derivation for the word elephant, 5 *n.*
GUILLIM, heraldry of the elephant, 38 *n.*

HAIRY elephants, 159 *n.*
Hardy, Colonel, story of, 69
Haroun, Alraschid, sends an elephant to Charlemagne, 35
[HA]RRISON, Dr., on the anatomy of the elephant, 26 *n.*, 57 *n.*, 60, 61
— on the structure of the head, 79
— on the ear of the elephant, 167
Hastisilpe, a Singhalese work on elephants, 17 *n.*, 21
Hawkus. *See* Hendoo, 155
Head, wound in, fatal, 79
— section of, 80
— this fact noticed by Pliny, 79 *n.*
Hearing. *See* Ear
Heber, Bishop, describes a diminutive species of elephant, 159 *n.*
Hedges, dreaded by elephants, 67
Height, exaggerated estimates of, in elephants, 30
Hendoo, used by the mahout, 155
Herd, the term described as applied to the elephant, 45
— similarity of features in, 45
— submissive to one leader, 50
— their conventional association and attachment, 45
HERODOTUS, account of the antipathy of the elephant to the camel, 13
— veneration for white horses and white oxen, 23
Himalayas, elephant paths on, 43
Hippopotamus, solitary individuals of, 49
HODGSON, Mr. B. H., his explorations in Nepal, ix.
Hog, double stomach of, 58
HOLLAND, DR., on the physiology of tusks, 17 *n.*
HOME, Sir EVERARD, on the double stomach of the elephant, 58
— on the ear of the elephant, 166, 167
HOME, RANDAL, his heraldry of the elephant, 38
HOOKER, Dr., elephants in the Himalayas, 43
Hora. *See* Rogue, 47, 72
HORACE, mentions a white elephant at Rome, 24
Horse, alleged antipathy of the elephant to, 12
— instances in disproof of this, 13
— killed by a trained elephant, 13
— anecdote of the meeting of a horse and an elephant, 19
— structure of the shoulder joint, 41

IDLENESS, love of, in tame elephants, 165
Indian elephant supposed to differ from that of Sumatra, vi.
— comparative anatomy of, vii.
— varieties of the same species in, x.
— elephant is dying out in India, 6 *n.*
Indicopleustes (*see* Cosmas), export of elephants, 5
Ivory, annual importations of, 6 *n.*
— proportion from Ceylon, 6 *n.*
— of Ceylon preferred in China, 6 *n.*
— African preferred in Europe, 6 *n.*
— weight of, in various countries, 8 *n.*
— immense African tusks at Goa, 8 *n.*
— how formed. *See* Dentine, 173

JAFFNA, instinct shown by elephants at, 64
Jardine, Sir William, fallacy as to elephants shedding tusks, 7 *n.*

Java, no elephants in the island, vi.
Joints, ancient error as to the elephant having none, 32
— explanation of its origin, 38, 39

KANDY, the King of, held the killing of an elephant a criminal offence, 5
— his hunts for capturing elephants, 96
Keddah. *See* Corral, 104
Kimbul-oya. *See* Alligator River, 106
Knox, his account of executions by trained elephants, 17
— on the attachment of the herd to the young, 47
— his accounts of elephant hunts in Kandy
Kombook tree; lime extracted from the bark, 110
Korahl. *See* Corral.
Korles, the Seven, elephant hunts in, 4
Kornegalle, beauty of the place, 107
— its temple the resort of Buddhists, 108
— sacred footstep on the rock, 108
Kraal. *See* Corral
— derivation of the word, 105
Kurahl. *See* Corral
Kurminia-galla, 107 *n.*
Kurunoi-galla. *See* Kornegalle

LABOUR of tame elephants too costly, 164, 174. *See* Tame Elephants
Lampongs. *See* Sumatra, viii.
Leap, the elephant unable to, 40
— anecdote, doubtful, of an elephant leaping, 41
LE BRUN, his account of the elephants in Ceylon, 5 *n.*
Leyden, elephants in Museum, x.
Life, duration of in the elephant, 177, 178
Lightning, dreaded by elephants, 68
Lindsay, Mr., adventure with elephants, 75
LIVINGSTONE, Dr., on the solitary hippopotamus, 49
Llama, double stomach of, 60 *n.*
Louis XIV., elephant belonging to, 57
Loxodon. *See* Elephas Sumatranus, vi.
Luca bos, Roman term for the elephants of Pyrrhus, 4 *n.*

MACCABEES, story of Jews killed by elephants, 16 *n.*, 154 *n.*
Machlis, an unknown animal, described by Pliny, 33
M'GEE, Dr., his account of flies hurrying towards persons dying, 139 *n.*
Mahawanse, mention of a white elephant in, 23
Mahout, elephant driver, the power of discrimination in India, x.
— conduct of the mahouts in a corral, 129
— mahouts said to die young, 166
Males, proportion of in a herd, small, 47
Malta, small fossil elephant found at, 159 *n.*
Man, elephant has no natural antipathy to, 10
— few deaths occasioned by them, 10
Manaar, singular scene on shipping elephants for India, 102
— described in A.D. 1701, 102
Marfil, Spanish name for ivory, 4 *n.*
— *See Mafirm*, Portuguese, ib.

Marfil, Palma de, the vegetable ivory palm, 4 *n.*
Marfim, Portuguese for ivory, 4 *n.*
MASSOUDI, on the use of the elephant in war, 159 *n.*
MATTHEW PARIS, his error as to the joints of the elephant, 36
Matura, elephants shipped from for India, 103
Mercer, Mr. Græme, story of a fight between two elephants, 16
Metatarsus, shortness of, enables the elephant to climb, 43
MOLYNEUX, his anatomy of the elephant, 56
Moormen of Ceylon, 97. *See* Panickeas.
MORRIS, Mr., conducts the corral in 1847, 109
MOULIN, A., his letter to Sir William Petty, 56 *n.*
"*Mudda.*" *See* "Must," 11
Muddy water not objected to by elephants, 55
Music, elephants' love of, 168
"Must," term explained, 11

NOUAER, size of African ivory at, 8 *n.*
NATIVES of Ceylon, their narratives of accidents and adventures with elephants, 71
Negombo, adventures with elephants at, 75
Nepal-root, a poison for elephants, 6
Nepal, mode of capturing elephants in, 97
Nile, White, enormous tusks got near, 8 *n.* *See* Baker, Sir Samuel
Noises produced by elephants, 27
Noosers. *See* Cooroowe, 122
— their extraordinary courage, 136
Noosing elephants, as practised by the Panickeas, 99
Noosing in a corral, operation described, 122, 124
Numidia, Medal of, 156 *n.*

OLFACTORY lobes, 26 *n.*
Optic nerve in the elephant, 26 *n.*
Osteology of the elephant. *See* Teeth, vi. x.
OWEN, Prof., on the anatomy of the elephant, 56 *n.*, 59, 60, 62
— on the formation of ivory, 173

PAIN, patient endurance of, 168
PALLEGOIX, on the white elephant, 23 *n.*
— on sounds produced by elephants, 30 *n.*
Palma de marfil, the vegetable ivory palm, 4 *n.*
Panickeas, their marvellous skill as trackers, 97
— their singular courage, 79
— their method of capturing wild elephants, 99
— mode of taming after capture, 101
— their method of conducting the captives to the coast, 101
PARIS. *See* MATTHEW PARIS.
Peccary, double stomach of, 58
PETHERICK, his account of large ivory in Soudan, 8 *n.*
PHILE, his error as to the joints of the elephant, 35
— difficulty of the elephant in rising, 30
— elephant does not object to muddy water, 55 *n.*
— thinks the elephant hates the pig, 117 *n.*
— on elephants as executioners, 154 *n.*
— elephant's love of music, 168 *n.*

PHILLIPE, on the supposed superiority of the Ceylon to the Indian elephant, 152
Physiologus. *See* THEROALDUS, 36
PICTET, Prof., his essay on the derivation of the word *elephant*, 4 *n.*
Pigs, antipathy of the elephant to. *See* Swine, 14
— spoil the capture at a corral, 116
Pingo, 71 *n.*
Pit-falls, elephants surprised in, 67
— objections to, 96
PLINY, his fallacy as to the elephant shedding his tusks, 7 *n.*
— as to the antipathy of the elephant to other animals, 15
— error as to the joints of the elephant, 32
— the *machlis*, 33
— terror of the elephant for white rods, 128
— mode of taming it, 151
— belief that the elephant has two hearts, 160
Poison for destroying elephants in Bengal, 6
POLYHISTOR. *See* SOLINUS, 35
Ponnekella. *See* Mahout, 122
Portuguese, elephant hunts conducted by, 95
— origin of the word corral, 105
POTT, conjecture as to the derivation of the word "elephant," 4 *n.*
PRINGLE, on power of elephant to uproot trees, 162 *n.*
Provençal song-writers, errors as to the elephant, 37
Pseudodoxia Epidemica. *See* Sir THOMAS BROWNE.
Ptolemy Philopater, employs elephant to kill Jewish martyrs, 16 *n.*
Punishments for tame elephants, 165
Puswael, a gigantic bean, 110
PYRARD, on the supposed superiority of the elephant of Ceylon to that of India, 152
Pyrrhus, his elephants, 4 *n.*, 150

RAIN, coming of foreseen by the elephant, 69
Raja-Kariya, 110. *See* Ripon.
Ramgur, method of poisoning elephants in, 6
Ranghani, the nooser, 123
— his prowess and success, 127
Raté-mahat-meyas, encourage the taking of elephants in corrals, 111
REINAUD, on the use of the elephant in war, 154 *n.*
Repose, peaceful, of the elephant, 84
Retirement, love of, 85
Rhinoceros, alleged antipathy between and the elephant, 9
Ripon, Earl of, abolishes raja-kariya, 110
Rise, difficulty of the elephant to, 38, 39
Rogers, Major, story of his horse and the elephants, 13 *n.*
— elephant shot by him falls on its knees, 39
— number killed by him, 77 *n.*
Rogue elephant, their origin and habits, 46
— their vice and depredations, 49, 50, 82 *n.*
— captured in a corral, 138
— his death, 138
Rome, performance of elephants, 168 *n.*, 183
Ronkedor. *See* Rogue, 47 *n.*
Ronquedue. *See* Rogue, ib.

SAGACITY of the elephant, its superiority questioned, 68
— Indian elephant said to excel the African in, 150
— compared with that of the horse and dog, 161
Saragossa, elephant fight, exhibited, 10 *n.*
SCHLEGEL, Prof., on the elephant of Sumatra, viii.
— doubts its distinctness from the elephant of Ceylon, viii.–xi.
— on the supposed superiority of the Ceylon to the Indian elephant, 152 *n.*
Serpents, in Ceylon, more accidents from than from elephants, 10
SEVERAC, JORDANUS DE, on the mode of training elephants in Cambodia, 157 *n.*
SHAKSPEARE, error as to the joints of the elephant, 37
— on capturing elephants in pitfalls, 96 *n.*
Shaw, fallacy as to the elephant shedding the tusks, 7 *n.*
Shilook, size of African ivory at, 83
Shooting elephants, 77
— cruelties of, 77 *n.*
— fatal spot in head, 79, and ear, ib.
Siam, elephant of, xi.
— sounds produced by, 30 *n.*
Sight, power of, 26
— accuracy of eye when working, 162
Silhet, elephant of, x.
Sinbad of the Sea, story of the burial place of dead elephants, 181
Siribeddi, the female decoy, her ability, 123
— her conduct, 145
Skinner, Major, story of his dog, 15
— his description of a strange sound made by elephants, 29
Skinner, Major, finds elephant traces on Adam's Peak, 41
— number of elephants shot by him, 78
— scene described by,—elephants at night, 51
— story of the courage of an elephant hunter, 99 *n.*
SLEAMAN, General, account of wolves suckling children, 47 *n.*
Sloane, Sir Hans, on the anatomy of the elephant, 56 *n.*
Smell, power of, 27, 98
SOLINUS, his error as to the joints of the elephant, 35
Sounds uttered by the elephant, 27
Soup, made from the elephant's foot, 89
Speed of an elephant, 32
Sport. *See* Shooting
Stomach of the elephant, double, 56
Stones, how raised by elephants, 162
STRACHAN, Mr., description of shipping elephants at Manaar, 103 *n.*
— on their liability to sudden death, 160 *n.*
Structure of the elephant, 4
STUCKLEY, Dr. WILLIAM, on the anatomy of the elephant, 56 *n.*
Sudden death, liability of elephants to, 159, 160 *n.*
"Sun and moon," emblems of duration, 187
Sumatra, elephant of, vi.
— called *gadjah*, vi.
— description by Temminck, *n.* vii.
— opinion of Prof. Schlegel on its distinctness from the elephant of India, viii.
— ribs and vertebræ, vii.
— teeth of, vi.
— this opinion controverted by Dr. Falconer, ix.

Surgical operations on elephants, 168
Swimming, action of the elephant in, 55
Swine, alleged antipathy of elephant to, 11, 14

TAME elephants, their conduct in the corral, 134. *See* Decoys
— value of their labour 162, 174
— levelling trees, 163
— piling timber, 164
— laziness, 165
— punishments, 165
— attachment to attendants, 166
— medical treatment, 168, 170
— obedience to orders, 169
— causes of death in captivity, 171
— weight of draught, 174
— cost of feeding a tame elephant, 175
— favourite food, 175
TAVERNIER, on the supposed superiority of the elephant of Ceylon, 153 *n.*
Teeth of the Sumatran elephant, vi.
TEMMINCK'S *Dutch Possessions in India*, vi.
— account of Sumatran elephant, viii.
THEROALDUS, *Physiologus*, error in, as to the joints of the elephant, 36
THEVENOT, on the supposed superiority of the Ceylon elephant to that of India, 152
THOMSON, error in his *Seasons*, as to the joints of the elephant, 38
Timber, how dragged by elephants, 161 *n.*, 162
— wonderful skill in piling of, 164
Tipperah, elephant of, x.
Tissaweva. *See* Anarajapoora, 65
Tooth-ache, 172
Training elephants, 150, &c.
— first employments, 161
— males more unmanageable than females, 158
— process of, 150
— varieties of disposition, 159
Trees, manner in which elephants level them, 146
— stories of overthrowing exaggerated, 162
Trompe. See Trunk
Trumpeting, peculiar sound of, 144
Trunk, so called from "trump," 28
— Aristotle compares the sound to a trumpet, ib.
— strange drawings of, in the fifteenth century, 28 *n.*
Tushes, their use to the elephant, 7
— they, and not the tusks, shed, 7 *n.*
Tuskers, influence of in the herd, 50
— their efficiency in a corral, 136
Tusks, rare in the Ceylon elephant, 6
— in Africa both male and female have them, 6
— average weight of those imported, 60 cwt., 6 *n.*
— in Ceylon are light, owing to the animals being shot young, 6 *n.*, 8
— a favourite treasure in Buddhist temples, 6 *n.*, 8
— both sexes have, in India and Africa, 6 *n.*, 8
— fallacy as to the elephant shedding his tusks, 7
— conjecture as to the presence of, in African elephant, and their absence in that of India and Ceylon, 7
— weight in various countries, 8 *n.*
— instance of a diseased one, 8 *n.* *See* Brooke, Sir Victor

Tusks, female elephant has none, in Ceylon, 9
— not ordinarily used as weapons of offence, 9
— fight between an elephant and two bulls, at Saragossa, 10 *n.*
— fight of two elephants with their tusks, 10
— story in Maccabees of Jews killed by elephants, 16 *n.*
— what is their use, 17, 17 *n.*
— abnormal varieties in shape, 17 *n.*
TYTLER, Mr., story of curiosity in elephants, 67 *n.*

VALENTYN, his account of shipping elephants for India from Ceylon, 103
Vegetable ivory palm, 4 *n.*
Vulgar Errors. *See* Sir THOMAS BROWNE, 32

WATER, love of the elephant for, 4 *n.*
— attempt to derive the word *elephant* from, 4 *n.*
— receptacle for, in the stomach, 56
— quantities withdrawn by the trunk in the corral, 133
Weber's *Metrical Romance* of the thirteenth century, 12 *n.*
Wells, dug by elephants, 54
White elephant; a lusus naturæ, 23
— exhibited in Holland in 1633, 24
— mentioned by Horace at Rome ib.
WHITE, GILBERT, of Selborne, on the affection of animals to the young of others, 46 *n.*
WILKINSON, Sir GARDNER, on the knowledge of the elephant in ancient Egypt, 152 *n.*
White oxen worshipped in Egypt, 23
WOLF, his strange adventures in Ceylon, 31 *n.*, 48, 105 *n.*
— on the capture of wild elephants, 96 *n.*
— on the height of the elephant, 31
Wolves suckling children, 46 *n.*
Wound of Lieut. Fretz, 90
WRIGHT'S *Reliquiæ Antiquæ*, 36

YOUNG, affection for, 47
Young elephants, their conduct when captured, 137
— their tricks in captivity, 138, 148
YULE, Colonel, on the liability of the elephant to sudden death, 160 *n.*